CHINA DIARY

CHINA DIARY

Sundeep Bhutoria

MACMILLAN

This edition first published in India 2019 by Pan
an imprint of Pan Macmillan Publishing India Private Limited,
707, Kailash Building
26 K. G. Marg, New Delhi – 110 001
www.panmacmillan.co.in

Pan Macmillan, 20 New Wharf Road, London N1 9RR
Basingstoke and Oxford
Associated companies throughout the world
www.panmacmillan.com

ISBN 978-93-89109-32-0

1 3 5 7 9 8 6 4 2

Typeset by Manmohan Kumar
Printed and bound in India by Thomson Press India Ltd.

To Manjari,
who suffers the most due to
my unlimited travel

CONTENTS

FOREWORD

I am the only Indian diplomat alive who spent two years in Mao Tse Tung's China. My interest in post 1949 China has never diminished. Mao radically changed the mindset of hundreds of millions, not only for his generation but also that of succeeding ones.

Sundeep Bhutoria's book is a record of the five days he spent in China between 22 May 2017 to 26 May. He travelled widely by plane, train, car and bus. He is a well-to-do Culturist from Kolkata, benignly infected by the travel bug.

I read his, "China Dairy" with great interest and pleasure. I was also impressed by his familiarity with China's history—past and present. I found his chapter on Xi'an and Xinjiang gripping and fascinating.

The Xi'an means "Western Peace". It is the starting point of the Silk Road and is now a tourist destination on account of the breath-taking Terracotta Warriors, accidentally discovered in 1974 by a farmer named Yang Xinmin.

Each one of the 8000 figures have a different facial expression. They survived the ravages of several thousand years.

A great example of the genius of the art master who created them. Thirty thousand Sunni Muslims reside in Xi'an.

The chapter on Xinjiang, the only Muslim majority part of China, is the hard core of the book. Xinjiang is a "festering wound" for which the People's Republic has found no solution.

The author gives lively accounts of the travels of Chinese Buddhists, Yuan Chwang, Fa-Hien and I. Tsing in the first millennium.

The relationship between Prime Minister Modi and President Xi Jinping is dealt in some detail. Differences have been papered over but China is weary of a strong and powerful India.

Sundeep Bhutoria's "China Diary" is a valuable and revealing book which throws critical light on little known but crucially significant aspects of the inscrutable character of the Chinese people.

Napoleon Bonaparte said that the 21st Century will be China's century. Let us wait and see.

K. Natwar Singh
Former Foreign Minister

PROLOGUE: THE BEGINNING OF MY JOURNEY

I am at Taj West End, Bengaluru, India. I checked in here on the night of 17 May 2018 on a month-long sabbatical as a lot of my creative work was due. Apart from a few other works, I wanted to pen my thoughts on China which I had visited exactly a year ago and scribbled my experiences in a diary. I also intend to write a book on leopards.

As election results are just out, Bengaluru and the whole state of Karnataka is politically charged up. Being one of the most strategically located hotels, Taj West End is a happening place and much in demand at present.

I usually spend my summers in St James Court, London, Buckingham Gate, another Taj property. London has been my summer sojourn for the past two decades; this one is a break from that. Both the properties of the Taj Group of Hotels are unique. The Gulmohar suite of Taj West End is more like a private bungalow with a lawn. Getting a booking at this time of the year comes with a stroke of luck.

This tranquil tropical paradise at the heart of Bengaluru is spread over twenty acres of lush green garden. British couple Mr and Mrs Bronson started this as a boarding house with 10 beds in 1887 and called it Bronson's West End. It only housed British soldiers and provided boarding with laundry and kitchen.

The popularity of the hotel grew and the property changed hands many times. The Taj Group bought it in 1984. This heritage building is located on high grounds, next to the Golf Club and adjacent to the Race Club. West End now has over a hundred magnificent rooms and suites with a gorgeous view. A stroll through the hotel's Art Corridor gives an idea of what Bengaluru was like during a gentler, elegant era not too long ago. A majestic red cast iron post box—oldest in the city—is still operational in this era of e-world.

The Corridor never ceases to awe. Pause for a moment and you would perhaps be staring at one of the oldest images of the Taj or maybe an artwork of exquisite beauty. Colonial history blends in with modern day luxury and hospitality in perfect harmony. Walk a while and you come to the 170-year-old famed rain tree from long before the hotel came into being. The other iconic structure, older than the hotel, is the Muneswara Temple which is open to the guests and the locals. Few steps further down the memory lane, a 100-year-old staircase ends up in a green abode—the grand Terrace Garden.

Voted India's best business hotel, my old acquaintance from Taj Bengal, Kolkata, Mr. Somnath Mukherjee is at the helm of Taj West End. His task is to ensure that the good going goes on. In fact, St James Court, Taj Hotel and Taj

West End technically come under my friend Prabhat Verma, who is undoubtedly one of the finest hoteliers professionally and keeps an eagle eye for details. Well known in the hotel industry, he has a Kolkata connect and is a frequent visitor and an ardent follower of Belur Math in Howrah, the headquarters of Rama Krishna Mission founded by Swami Vivekananda.

For me, this hotel is a perfect getaway from the world of mobiles, emails, and twitters. I can, though, sense the politically surcharged atmosphere as many political bigwigs are also staying here. Scores of photographers and journalists at the gates and a posse of security men have somewhat dampened the solitude that I hoped for. However, I know it will soon pass.

As I settle down into the comfortable environs of Taj West End here on this day of 22 May 2018, I remember exactly a year ago on this hot summer day I had landed in China for a five-day visit with an Indian delegation. I was all geared up for my summer sojourn in London, but this was a scheduled detour. A visit that was memorable in many ways. Besides a sneak peek into the humongous economic development and urbanization that China had unleashed, I also met some of the very talented artists of China and some Indians who have made China their second home.

DAY 1

(22 May 2017)

I had first visited The People's Republic of China in 2003, as a member of a goodwill delegation of the Indian Federation of the United Nations Associations (IFUNA). The delegation was led by veteran Indian politician Ram Niwas Mirdha, a Member of Parliament (MP) from Tamil Nadu, a minister from the Government of West Bengal and two others were a part of this group.

Once again, after almost 14 years, I am in China on a five-day trip. I hope to know more about this ancient civilization and the modern economic dynamo; the art and culture and the humongous structural changes that continue at breakneck speed.

How distinct China is from the rest of the world!

This is a common feeling that begins to seep in from the very moment you step out of the plane.

I am visiting China at a time when it is making global headlines. I am here on an invitation from the Beijing-based United Nations Association-China (UNA-China) which is the only non-governmental organization in China promoting the purposes and principles of the United Nations as enshrined in its Charter. The membership is open to the general public and social entities that are enthusiastic about the cause of the UN. UNA-China's Council consists of former senior diplomats with extensive experience in the UN, renowned scholars who specialize in UN studies, and entrepreneurs who are keen on promoting the cause of the UN.

This time our delegation is lead by Dikanchi D Shira, wife of Meghalaya Chief Minister Mukul Sangma. D Shira is a Member of the Legislative Assembly (MLA) of Meghalaya, one of India's seven-sister states of the northeast.

I am the deputy leader of the delegation. The other members of the delegation are Chander Prakash Mahajan, a representative from Himachal Pradesh and a member of the UNA, Vinayak Srivastav, Rakchira Dalbot Shira and Meenakshi Verma from IFUNA.

United Nations Associations (UNAs)

UNAs are national civil society organizations that provide a link between the citizens of the world and the United Nations (UN) by seeking to ensure that the UN is relevant to the lives of the people it exists to serve. UNAs have different programs and a variety of constituencies, such as individual members, member organizations, and partner schools and universities. IFUNA is the Indian unit of the World Federation of United Nations Associations (WFUNA).

World Federation of United Nations Associations (WFUNA): WFUNA, a global nonprofit organization representing and coordinating a membership of over 100 national UNAs and their thousands of constituents, was started in 1946 under Article 60 of the Swiss Civil Code.

WFUNA works to strengthen and improve the UN by engaging people who share a global mindset—global citizens—and support international cooperation. The WFUNA's Secretariat is based in One UN Plaza in New York City and at the Palais des Nations in Geneva, Switzerland.

WFUNA is an independent, non-governmental organization with Category One Consultative Status at the Economic and Social Council (ECOSOC); Associate Status with the United Nations Department of Public Information (DPI) and United Nations Organization for Education Science and Culture (UNESCO); Special List with the UN International Labor Organization (ILO); General Status with the UN Conference on Trade and Development (UNCTAD); Status with UN Food and Agricultural Organization (FAO), International Atomic and Energy Agency (IAEA), United Nations Children's Fund (UNICEF), UN World Meteorological Association and consultative or liaison links with many other UN organizations and agencies. WFUNA is a nonprofit organization under Section 501(c)(3) of the United States Internal Revenue Service Code.

I currently serve as the Treasurer of WFUNA. During its history, WFUNA has served as a forum for global dialogues on development. Several suggestions, like the establishment of an Economic Commission for Africa, were first adopted at WFUNA Plenary Assemblies and then endorsed by the governments. In 2015, UNAs around the world embraced the 2030 Agenda, and gave the Sustainable Development Goals (SDGs) a high priority on their agendas.

WFUNA has actively supported reform of the UN and its capacity to meet new tasks and challenges. In 2016, it launched historic Security Council Election Debates with candidates competing for non-permanent seats.

WFUNA Foundation is another organization headquartered in Kolkata. The Foundation, launched by Foreign Minister Sushma Swaraj in March 2015, has five advisors and four trustees, me being one of them. The purpose of this Foundation is to further the activities, initiatives and programs of WFUNA in India so as to spread awareness on issues such as human rights, sustainable development and others.

Coming back to UNA, there is a branch of the UNA in 18 Indian states which include West Bengal, Maharashtra, Tamil Nadu, Orissa, Punjab, Meghalaya, Assam, Andhra Pradesh, Uttar Pradesh and others. These branches work for common goals as per the guidelines of the Indian Federation of the United Nations Associations (IFUNA) under the aegis of WFUNA.

The administrative functioning of the Indian UNA and the Chinese UNA is very different. While the IFUNA administration is managed, run and controlled by the civil society, its Chinese counterpart is by and large an organization of diplomats and senior bureaucrats appointed by the Foreign Ministry of the Republic of China. The office of UNA China is housed in one of the foreign affairs premises of China.

I must state here that the affiliation fees of the IFUNA is paid by the Ministry of External Affairs of India and they do give grants to IFUNA which works independently and like a non-governmental organization (NGO).

Besides major administrative and functional differences between the UNAs of India and China, there is a bilateral agreement between both the UNAs on the basis of which delegations visit each other every alternate year.

I was fortunate enough to get selected to be a part of that delegation that visited China in 2003. I had learned a lot in the great company of Shri Ram Niwas Mirdha. There are so many unforgettable shared memories of that trip to China with Sri Mirdha. I would recount one that revealed his immense popularity and respect among others.

During that trip in 2003, the Chinese officials took our delegation led by Sri Mirdha to visit a diamond factory of a leading industrialist. On our way to the factory, the Chinese officials lavished praises on the industrialist who is of Indian origin. Someone who made it big in a very short time. On reaching the factory, the industrialist, who the Chinese officials were praising no end, graciously touched the feet of Sri Mirdha and softly asked, 'Sir, do you remember me?'

Sri Mirdhaji said 'No!'

The industrialist said, '25 years ago, I was your chauffeur on duty when you visited the United States. You only had advised me to start my own business. And here I am.'

We all stood speechless.

I remembered during my first visit to China, I had visited a park where I saw the bust of Kavi Guru Rabindranath Tagore. Tagore had visited China in 1924 and 1928 and had stayed there for several months during his first visit. He visited Shanghai and stayed in Peiping where he delivered many public lectures supported by the Shang Chih Hsueh Hui (Aspiration Society) of Peiping.

Tagore's works 'The Crescent Moon' and 'China' were translated in Chinese which greatly inspired the then outstanding poet of China Hsu Chih-mo and his friends who formed the Crescent Moon Society in Shanghai along with Crescent Moon Bookstore and magazines. Tagore celebrated his 64th Birthday in 1924 in Peiping and his play 'Chitra' was staged in English. Hsu along with his colleagues Lin Chang-min and his daughter Lin Hui-ying acted in the play. Tagore was greatly moved by their gesture and was perhaps one of his happiest moments in China.

However, it wasn't all milk and honey. Tagore also had his sad moments when youths of Communist Party of China had opposed his lectures and distributed uncomplimentary leaflets in the lecture halls.

After so many years, I am once again visiting China as the Deputy Leader of a delegation. It is quite natural for me to delve into the memories of so many great men and women of India who had visited China and left their indelible mark.

It was noon when I landed at the Beijing International Airport on 22 May 2017 via Hong Kong, the Chinese special administrative region. The whole world had come to know about the rift between India and China on One Belt One Road (OBOR) with India refusing to be a part of the initiative. OBOR was a topic of discussion in the diplomatic and political circles and had set tongues wagging, often leading to impassioned discussions during parties and coffee table talks.

Hong Kong

I have visited so many countries in almost all the continents far away from India. Though strangely, I am yet to visit Bangladesh which is our next door neighbour and also Hong Kong. I flew by Dragon Airways with a transit at the Hong Kong airport. This was the first time I had set foot in Hong Kong. The Hong Kong airport is very well planned and every gate has a lounge in numerical and alphabetical order.

Archaeological findings suggest human activity in Hong Kong dates back over 30,000 years. Stone tools from the Old Stone Age have been excavated in Sai Kung and Wong Tei Tung. The territory that now comprises Hong Kong was incorporated into China during the Qin dynasty (221–206 BC), and the area was firmly consolidated under the ancient kingdom of Nanyue (203–111 BC). Emperor Qin Shi Huang founded the Qin dynasty which is considered to be the first dynasty of Imperial China named after its heartland in Qin state.

The population of Hong Kong began to increase under the Han dynasty (206 BC–AD 220) which was the second Imperial dynasty. Spanning over four centuries, the Han period is considered a golden age in Chinese history. To this day, China's majority ethnic group refers to themselves as the 'Han Chinese' and the Chinese script is referred to as 'Han characters.'

Hong Kong and its New Territories served as a port, naval base, salt production centre and later as a base for the exploitation of pearls under the Tang dynasty. The New Territories, Hong Kong Island, and the Kowloon Peninsula are the three main regions of Hong Kong covering over 85% of the territory and home to half of the population.

In 1276, during the Mongol invasion, Hong Kong saw its first population boom as Chinese refugees entered the area driven by war and famine. Others arrived seeking employment. Britain occupied the island of Hong Kong on 25 January 1841 and used it as a military outpost. China was defeated and forced to cede Hong Kong to Britain in the Treaty of Nanjing signed on 29 August 1842. Later, with the Convention of Beijing Treaty in 1860 Kowloon was ceded to crown. Again in 1898 the Chinese and British signed the Second Convention of Beijing Treaty which gave a 99-year lease agreement for the nearly 200 islands surrounding Hong Kong called the 'New

Territories' to the British. In return, China got a promise that the islands would be returned to it after 99 years.

Hong Kong was occupied by Japan from 23 December 1941 to 15 August 1945. By the end of the Second World War in 1945, Hong Kong had been liberated by joint British and Chinese troops. However, the population of Hong Kong under Japanese rule had shrunk to 600,000 from a pre-war population of 1.6 million due to the scarcity of food and emigration.

Hong Kong outlasted most other British colonies. Britain never had a clear policy on Hong Kong and applied its own jurisprudence and justice system to set and implement standards irrespective of the fact whether it was relevant or worked at all. After the Second World War, the British Empire lost its global power status and gave up most of its colonies including the British Commonwealth. However, the colonial status lingered on in Hong Kong and China did not make an issue of it until the 1980s.

On December 19, 1984, British Prime Minister Margaret Thatcher and Chinese Premier Zhao Ziyang signed the Sino-British Joint Declaration, in which Britain agreed to return the New Territories, Kowloon and Hong Kong itself when the 99-year lease term expired. China promised to implement a 'One Country, Two Systems' regime, under which for 50 years Hong Kong citizens could continue to practice capitalism and political freedoms forbidden on the mainland. On July 1, 1997, the lease ended and the government of Great Britain transferred control of Hong Kong and surrounding territories to the People's Republic of China. Since then, Hong Kong is a Special Administrative Region of China.

Jianguo Hotel Beijing

Coming back to my first day in Beijing, the other members of the Indian delegation reached Beijing from Delhi in the evening a few hours after my arrival from Kolkata. I checked in at the Jianguo Hotel arranged by our host. The hotel is

FIGURE 1.1: Jianguo Hotel Beijing

considered a classic hotel in Beijing located adjacent to the Beijing diplomatic quarter in the heart of the city's central business district (CBD).

Jianguo Hotel Beijing is the first joint-venture hotel in China since 1982 and the only hotel in Beijing built around a traditional water garden with a courtyard, fountains and carved figures of lions in stone. Natural light streams in through the glass ceiling adorned by a white-marble lobby with brass chandeliers. A French restaurant and a cafe overlooking the garden serving international and local cuisines. A classical harpist plays music in the evenings. Lavish business centres, conference rooms, swimming pool, fitness facility, acupuncture and massage treatment rooms are in the offing.The famous silk market is just a few minutes walk while the famous Tiananmen Square takes a 10-minute ride by a car to reach. Other historical sights are also located close by. The Chinese Foreign Ministry prefers to put up their international delegates at this hotel.

The week I landed in China was quite an important week in terms of India–China relations. A couple of days before I left Kolkata, the Consul General of the People's Republic of China in Kolkata, MA Zhanwu, made a press statement. It was on 19 May 2017 and the media session was held at the leading five-star hotel in Kolkata, The Oberoi Grand. The Chinese consulates have been spending a lot to get publicity in India and elsewhere. This is a part of its global campaign to develop soft power and carry out the state's propaganda campaigns.

MA Zhanwu shared details of the recently concluded Belt Road Initiative Forum (BRF) for International Cooperation held in Beijing on 14–15 May 2017. MA Zhanwu had, at the press briefing, remarked that BRF was a significant conference not only for China but also for Asia and the whole world and would be remembered as a major event in the international relations in the 21st century.

MA Zhanwu shared the vision of President Xi Jinping and said that the Belt and Road Initiative represents the spirit of the ancient silk road, which features peace and

FIGURE 1.2: Sundeep Bhutoria and MA Zhanwu, Consul General of the People's Republic of China in Kolkata

cooperation, openness and inclusiveness, mutual learning and mutual benefit. He indicated that this initiative emphasizes the achievement of synergy by combining the development strategies of different countries.

On the question regarding China Pakistan Economic Corridor (CPEC), Zhanwu said that CPEC was agreed upon by the governments of the two countries for the benefit of the two sides and the relevant projects have already started, but it is not targeted against any third country. He also said that China's position on the question of Kashmir is consistent and clear and CPEC development does not affect its position, and China believes that it is a dispute between India and Pakistan left from the past, and it is up to the two countries to sort it out through peaceful dialogue. He further added that the Belt Road Initiative (BRI) is aimed at converging rather than overriding the existing plans such as BCIM (Bangladesh China India Myanmar) and Look East Policy.

The Indian government neither believes or accepts this narrative. In fact, many of my friends in the Indian diplomatic circles have told me informally that all these 'sweet talks' conceal a global Chinese military strategy that is fraught with widespread geopolitical ramifications in the region. Given the timing of our visit to China, I knew from the very outset that OBOR of China, a hot topic, would crop up in meetings with our Chinese counterparts. More so, because of India's reluctance to be a party to it.

By the time I checked into the Hotel, my taste buds were craving for Indian food. I found the solution within walking distance of my hotel and in the food court of a mall. A good vegetarian platter of *samosa*, lentils, *naan*, and *paneer* was enough to satiate my Indian palate. I have realized that a wide variety of Indian food you get around the world is very extreme. Some are simply fabulous and make me wonder why these aren't available in India. While others are just unpalatable and forgettable. I have come across many Indian or fusion Indian restaurants overseas where the Indian food is worth dying for.

Figure 1.3: Indian Restaurant *Mirch Masala*

Bharat and Gita

After having Indian food at the food court I went to meet Bharat—an Indian artist settled in Beijing. Whenever I visit any country, I always make an earnest effort to meet up with the prominent non-resident Indians (NRIs) and also those local artists who have an abiding interest in fine arts, culture, and literature.

Bharat came to meet me with his sister Gita. Meeting Bharat and Gita was quite a revelation. My friend Arun Maheshwari of Vani Publishers had introduced me to them earlier. Though, I got to know about them and their splendid work only after meeting in person.

The sibling duo has a heart of gold and is among the finest persons I have ever met in my life. Their warmth and hospitality is infectious and can put anyone at ease. They were solely instrumental in making it possible for us to meet some of the Chinese artists of international repute, and some prominent Indians in Beijing.

Figure 1.4: Meeting Bharat and Gita

The duo, Bharat Singh and Gita aka Gurjinder, are sculptor artistes by profession. Their B&G Art Studio in Songzhuang, Beijing, is located in the largest art zone in the world. They came to China on scholarships and went on to earn a name and fortune for themselves. Their work of art has spread to over 20 countries. Though they have sculpted on the ice and other forms, most of their sculptural work is in bronze and based on themes of love, peace, friendship, kindness, music, nature or any issues of global concern that call for raising awareness.

The artworks unveiled at different exhibitions touch a chord with the audience and have been acquired by museums, galleries, and private collectors from around the world including the United States, United Kingdom, Japan, Canada, Spain, China, India, Malaysia, Korea, and other countries. In China, their work has been featured prominently in Beijing, Harbin, Changchun, Datong, Qingdao, Xiamen, Xuzhou, and Foshan.

For Bharat, it was love at first sight with Beijing when he arrived in 2000 on a Chinese Government Scholarship. Prior to that, he got his BA and MA degrees in fine arts from College of Art, Delhi. Bharat was a PhD research student of Professor Qian Shao Wu, a well-established Chinese sculptor at the Central Academy of Fine Arts in Beijing. Bharat developed an interest in drawing and the other arts when he was five years old. He received his PhD from the Central Academy. He calls Beijing his second home.

Gita also had a similar journey like her brother. She too graduated from College of Art, Delhi, where she received her Bachelor in Fine Arts (BFA) and Masters in Fine Arts (MFA) degrees in sculpture, in 2001 and 2004 respectively. She then came to Beijing via Chinese Government Scholarship in 2008 after getting her MFA in painting at Jiwaji University. She obtained her third MFA degree from the Central Academy of Fine Arts in Beijing. She also speaks Chinese fluently like her elder brother. Gita's artwork is an expression of her memories, dreams, desires, and reminiscences from her childhood—the joyful aspects of life. The siblings, who appeared in the 2011 Chinese hit TV series *Xia Nan Yang*, hope to push their creative boundaries and spread joy through their artwork.

My wish to meet a prominent Chinese artist on short notice was a challenging task for Bharat and Gita. I had to leave for Xi'an city on 24 May and my prior appointments kept me busy till 4 pm on 23 May. Bharat and Gita were unfazed and said they would try their best.

After meeting Bharat and Gita, I left for a meeting with the newly appointed Vice-President & Director General of UNA-China, Ms Zhang Dan, in my capacity as Treasurer of WFUNA.

Ms Zhang Dan has had wide experience in key positions. She joined the Ministry of Foreign Affairs of the People's Republic of China in 1990 where she worked as a third secretary, second secretary, and director of APEC division of the Department of International Organizations of the

Foreign Ministry. From 1997 to 2000, she worked in the Commissioner's Office of the Foreign Ministry of China in Hong Kong SAR. She was the Counsellor in the Mission of China to the United Nations in New York from 2006 till 2011 and was responsible for human rights, gender equality, and development related issues. From 2011 till 2014, she was in charge of international economic and development cooperation in the newly created Department of International Economic Affairs of the Foreign Ministry.

Ms Zhang Dan is an expert in China's participation in the United Nations. Working among 193 member states of the UN and the Secretariat since 2006, she managed a broad range of matters enabling effective and strategic participation of China at the United Nations. She has led many Chinese delegations and also served as the Vice-Chair and Rapporteur of the 46th Session of CSocD of UN.

UNA-China dinner

The Indian delegation flight from Delhi was delayed and it was obvious they would be late for the formal dinner at 7 pm hosted by Ambassador Lu Shumin, President of UNA-China, at the UNA Secretariat, Beijing.

At 5 pm, Zhang Yi, Deputy Director, UNA-China, whom I had met before at a WFUNA meeting came to pick me up from the hotel. We went to the office of UNA-China. As soon as I entered, I remembered my first visit to that office 14 years ago. After a one-on-one meeting with Zhang Dan, I met the Ambassador, Lu Shumin, President of UNA-China. By then, the Indian delegation had also arrived.

Ambassador Lu Shumin was born in Shaanxi Province of China and has held many important positions in foreign affairs in North America. He was the Counsellor in Chinese Embassy in the USA for four years. He also had stints in Indonesia and worked as the Vice President of the Chinese People's Institute of Foreign Affairs.

The official dinner started half an hour late at 7.30 pm. IFUNA, factoring in the flight timings, had requested the dinner for 7 pm. A formal Chinese dinner usually takes long. Food and dumplings are served in nicely decorated small dishes. One gets the feeling of eating out of jewellery boxes. A vegetarian meal was specially cooked for me. Twenty or

Figure 1.5: From Left to Right: Rakchira Dalbot Shira, Meenakshi Verma, Vinayak Srivastava, Dikanchi D Shira, Chander Prakash Mahajan, Ambassador Lu Shumin, Zhang Dan, Sundeep Bhutoria and LI Nan

more dishes were served to us over six or seven courses. I could only manage to eat a plum tomato juice and some potatoes.

OBOR and India

While I was preparing for my trip, China's OBOR, rechristened BRI, was making headlines all over the world. The Chinese government calls the initiative a bid to enhance regional connectivity and embrace a bright future, while critics say it is a push by China to take a larger role in global affairs with a China-centered trading network.

During the dinner, the topic of OBOR once again surfaced and both the sides treated it rather diplomatically. The Indian delegation was more ears than the tongue. As this topic would come up every now and then, and given its potential global significance, let me share some details. The Chinese initiative is to have six major highways-railways-ports-linked economic corridors connecting different continents. It was earlier in general terms called the Silk Route. China initiated a two-day conference on 15 and 16 May 2017, called the BRI which was attended by representatives of 60 countries and 30 heads of state.

India and Bhutan did not attend BRI because India had reservations in one of the USD 40 billion proposed investment corridors called CPEC which aims to connect Gwadar port in Pakistan to Kashghar in Xinxiang province via Balochistan, touching Pakistan's Federally Administered Tribal Area (FATA), Gilgit Baltistan and passing through

Pakistan Occupied Kashmir (PoK). India feels this is disputed territory and objects to the project passing through it because it would reinstate Pakistan's claim of sovereignty in the disputed area. CPEC is seen as a project that would be completed in the next 25 to 30 years.

Gwadar port in the Arabian Sea is located in Balochistan province of Pakistan. A section of the Baloch population is against the project which they feel is benefiting outsiders. Pakistan blames India alleging that India's intelligence wing RAW is fomenting unrest in the region. India strongly denies this.

As a trade route, CPEC would reduce drastically the time taken by Chinese goods, especially crude oil, to reach China through the long 12,000 to 13,000 kilometres journey via Strait of Malacca to the South China Sea. This corridor would reduce the cost and time of carrying goods from West Asia to China.

In Pakistan, many people feel there is a total lack of transparency on CPEC. Nobody, including leading institutions and think tanks, knows the details and the terms and conditions on which Pakistan is allowing China to invest. Others say the USD 40 billion China will invest under CPEC in Pakistan is more in the form of loans to Pakistan and not as a foreign direct investment. Some reports say these loans are repayable at a very high undisclosed rate of interest.

World Bank has warned Pakistan of the loans it has taken to reach a dangerous level by 2020 and Pakistan may find it difficult to pay back the interest accruing on these loans.

With fresh loans at high interest from China, the situation will be worse. Many in Pakistan are saying that the CPEC is a modern version of East India Company which will eventually lead to China controlling all aspects of Pakistan as the latter would have to service the debts on loans taken.

Indian establishment sees CPEC as not just an economic corridor but also a strategic move with defence and security implications in the region. India feels it will lead to the establishment of a strong Chinese military base in Pakistan.

India, in a counter strategy, is building Chabahar port in Iran on the Arabian Sea. Chabahar is some 70 kilometres from Gwadar. This will, in the long run, give Indian military a base to operate and protect its interest and also provide an alternative route to supply goods and materials to Afghanistan which does not have any border with India. Pakistan refuses to allow India to do transit trade with landlocked Afghanistan through its territory.

Indian government sees the Belt Road Initiative as a strategy to expand the zone of Chinese influence backed by military power. The Chinese government has been using its soft power to gain more and more countries to become a party to these projects. India, so far, been conspicuous by its absence.

Thus, the topic of OBOR is a hot potato and will continue to be so as far as India is concerned.

DAY 2

(23 May 2017)

On 23 May 2017, our second day in China, we started the day with a scheduled meeting with the scholars of China Institute of International Studies (CIIS) at their premises at 10 am.

China Institute of International Studies (CIIS)

The CIIS was founded in 1956 in its earlier avatar as the Institute of International Relations of the Chinese Academy of Sciences. It got its present name in 1986. The CIIS is the think tank of China's Ministry of Foreign Affairs and is directly administered by it.

CIIS carries out extensive research and analysis on a wide range of foreign policy issues mainly concerned with global politics and economy and also facilitates the decision-making process of the central government. In 1998, the ambit of CIIS expanded with the incorporation of China Center for International Affairs, formerly a research institution of China's State Council.

Figure 2.1: Author at CIIS

CIIS primarily focuses on issues concerning international politics and world economy and their medium and long-term impact. It includes comments and policy recommendations on the world's major events and burning issues.

The Institute hosts various seminars, conferences, scholarly discourses, and exchange programs throughout the year. This effort of the Institute is supported by over 100 researchers and other professionals including senior diplomats, area-study specialists, and pre-eminent experts in major fields of foreign affairs. The young scholars at the Institute are graduates with university degrees in International Relations and allied disciplines.

CIIS has been very active in publishing in English various reports and research findings to the foreign policymakers and institutions. It publishes books, periodicals, and articles on a regular basis though with a caveat that says that the views expressed in the publications are those of the authors not representing CIIS. Foreign affairs experts from outside China also contribute regularly to the think tank and its journal called *International Studies* which has a bi-monthly English edition. Our delegation was part of a program to exchange ideas and strengthen friendly relations.

CIIS has eight departments and four affiliate bodies namely, Department of Global Strategy, Information and Contingencies Analysis, American Studies, Asia-Pacific Security and Cooperation, EU Studies, Developing Countries Studies, Shanghai Cooperation Organization Studies, World Economy and Development Studies. The four affiliate bodies of CIIS are China National Commission for Pacific Economic Cooperation, China Commission of the Council for Security Cooperation in the Asia Pacific, China International Studies and Academic Exchange Foundation and China Arms Control and Disarmament Association.

Besides, there are Research Centers focused respectively on the study of the European Union, the Middle East, the South Pacific, China's Energy Strategy, Periphery Security and World Economy and Security.

At the CIIS, we had a meeting with the scholars Lan Jianxue and Tang Qifang. During the entire meeting, the Chinese representatives lavished praises on Prime Minister Narendra Modi and his policies. They told us how China has learned new and positive things from India.

Figure 2.2: TANG Qifang and LAN Jianxue of China Institute of International Studies (CIIS) and Dikanchi D Shira and Sundeep Bhutoria (from left to right)

They did tell us about OBOR and tried to convince us how it was good for the whole world, especially India. We had decided that we would not get into this topic which had generated controversy in India. The Indian government had stayed away from a very big International conclave hosted in Beijing, a week prior to our visit with representatives from more than 30 countries attending it. We gave our Chinese friends a patient hearing but refrained from making any statements or comments. One of the major issues with India is the CPEC project which India has condemned as being controversial involving disputed territories.

Just as we came out of the CIIS premises, I got a call from Bharat. He said he had managed to fix up a few appointments as I had requested. He said he was on his way to come and pick me up from the hotel. As we were scheduled to visit the Forbidden City and the Beijing Planning Exhibition Hall as a part of our itinerary, I had to take a call. Since I had visited both these places earlier, I decided that after my meeting at the Indian Mission, I would go with Bharat and meet up the artists with whom he had fixed up appointments in such a short time.

Forbidden City, Beijing

The Forbidden City (Zi Jin Cheng) is a palace complex in central Beijing spread over 178 acres. It is the world's largest palace complex with 980 buildings, Palace Museum, fourteen major gates, scores of gardens, courtyards, *hutongs* (alleys), and moats.

The UN declared Forbidden City as a World UN Heritage Site in 1987 for its traditional Chinese palace architecture housing 1.8 million artefacts. UNESCO has listed it as the largest collection of preserved ancient wooden structures in the world. Since 1925, the Forbidden City has been under the charge of the Palace Museum, another iconic institution.

The name Forbidden City or Zi Jin Cheng is derived from the Chinese name Zi, which, according to Chinese Astrology, alludes to the Pole Star considered the heavenly abode of the Celestial Emperor. The second part of the name Jin refers to the fact that no one could enter or leave the Palace without the Emperor's permission while the third part of the name Cheng means city.

For first time visitors, going around Forbidden City would be a tall task without a guide. Every year 16 million people come to visit this city. The Palace Museum has an impressive collection of artefacts which includes paintings, rare books, historical documents, ceramics, porcelain, brassware, seals, sculptures enamel works and many Chinese cultural relics. It also has the largest collection of timepieces of 18th and 19th centuries. During the 1933 Japanese invasion of China, national treasures were evacuated to Taiwan. Today, the site is commonly known as Gugong in Chinese meaning 'Former Palace.'

It took 14 years to build the City (1420–1402 BC) under the Ming dynasty after Chinese Emperor Zhu Di shifted China's capital from Nanjing to Beijing. Twenty-four consecutive Emperors of Ming and Qing dynasty ruled China from the precincts of this City till 1912. It served as their home and household as well as the ceremonial and political centre of the Chinese government for nearly 500 years. The Forbidden City is in the shape of a rectangle running 961 metres north to south to 753 metres east to west. A walled section of the city is called the Imperial City. The walls are 26 feet high.

The design of the Forbidden City reflected the philosophical and religious principles as well as the majesty of the emperors. The Palace architecture of the walled complex adheres to the traditional Chinese geomantic practice of *feng shui*. An importance of a building can be judged by its architectural style, number of figurines placed on the ridge of the roof and the colour of the roofs. Most roofs have yellow glazed tiles which represented the colour of the emperor.

After 1949 when Mao Zedong came to power, Beijing (the then Peking) was surrounded by 25 miles of walls and 16 multistoried gates guarded by stone lions. The Forbidden City is enclosed by a 20-feet deep moat and surrounded by other palaces and gardens. Beyond its walls, commemorative archways stretched across streets and a maze of hutongs lead to houses with central courtyards.

As a result of Mao's dictum 'make the past serve the present,' many historical areas south of the Forbidden City were razed to give way to the Great Hall of the People, the National Museum and the Tiananmen Square expansion. During the construction of Beijing's first subway line, many walls from the Ming era were destroyed. During the Cultural Revolution, historic sites were further destroyed. The Palace Museum was protected but a sign put up by the government called it 'A Palace of Blood and Tears.'

The process has now been reversed with the enactment of the 'Law for the Protection of Cultural Heritage of the People's Republic of China.' China now promotes the Palace Museum as a National Cultural Institution. China has initiated a 16-year project work to restore the Palace Museum to its pre-1912 state.

There was a controversy over the housing of popular café chain Starbucks in the Forbidden City. This outlet was shut in 2008 and replaced by a state-run café.

Gong De Lin Vegetarian Restaurant

Lunch was arranged by our hosts at the Gong De Lin Restaurant—the first vegetarian restaurant of Beijing—established in 1922, located a mile away from southern Tiananmen Square. After reaching the restaurant, I realized that this was more expensive than its non-vegetarian counterparts in the city.

The restaurant takes its name from Buddha doctrine 'Gradually accumulate benediction to the extent as the vast green forest covers the earth universal.' The name means—to spare no effort in benefiting the people's heart and soul. Gong De Lin is the only food restaurant in Beijing to serve a net-Buddhist cuisine and graded as the national first-class restaurant now. The restaurant plaque is written by Zhao Puchu, the President of the Buddhist Association of China.

In India, nearly half of the population is vegetarian with vegetarianism rooted in religion and culture. China, on the other hand, is the world's largest market for beef, pork, and poultry. And Beijing is no different. Until very recently, vegetarian restaurants were a rarity in Beijing. Though, I am told more and more Chinese are turning vegetarian with vegetarian eateries mushrooming across cities of China. A new dietary guideline issued by China's health industry a few years ago also suggested eating less meat, poultry and seafood. More and more young Chinese are embracing vegetarianism and the country's meat imports are on the decline.

Gong De Lin is a culture shock for many Indians. The restaurant's unique dishes never ceases to shock and surprise. One of the reasons for its steep price is that this eatery uses imitation meat, which are actually vegetarian ingredients, to produce classic Chinese-styled dishes such as pork, fish, and duck with uncanny resemblance and taste. The main dining hall is downstairs, with three private themed dining rooms occupying the upper level. Beer, wine spirits are available. This restaurant was full and we could make out that a table was possible through prior booking.

Here, vegetarian cooking has taken an art form and was more about imitating meat. Strict veggie-lovers will find dishes such as recreated chicken feet, imitation duck and shrimp entrees, and so on. The raw materials adopt the three kinds of mushrooms; six kinds of fungus including white and black fungus; fresh fruits and vegetables and processed food products made of soyabean. It totally relies on the super chefs' cooking techniques to create courses of dishes that are delicious, rich in nutrient, exquisitely styled, and completely mistaken for meat or fish.

Some of the recommended dishes are mixed vegetables in eighteen kinds; braised square bean curds with cole in red sauce; Indian vegetarian food; braised abalone with purple vegetables;

sauteed aloes with gingko; steamed fermented pieces of sticky, flexible, crystal flour; steamed bun with vegetable-stuffing and others. They all are exceptionally popular.

Some of the non-vegetarian members of our delegation were taken aback and confirmed that the entire meal actually tasted like non-vegetarian food. I felt amused by the fact that China had earned a copycat reputation worldwide for its ability to replicate electronic goods and gadgets. However, the fact that this talent extends to the domain of foodstuffs became known to us only after we stepped into this restaurant for a firsthand experience.

Beijing has quite a few Indian restaurants. The popular ones are *Mirch Masala, Ganges Indian, Swagat Indian, Indian Pavilion* and *Hazara.*

India Mission visit

From Gong De Lin we went to the Indian embassy for a meeting with Ambassador, Vijay Gokhale and other officials. I had met Mr Gokhale when he was the High Commissioner of India to Malaysia. I had attended the Republic Day function in Kuala Lumpur with him and also witnessed his immense popularity among the Indian diaspora in Kuala Lumpur.

When we reached the Indian Mission, the tension between the two nations was quite palpable. The Chinese officials accompanying our group decided not to enter the Mission and neither were the Indian Mission officials keen to have them in. It was a good round of closed-door meeting with Vijay Gokhale and other officials.

From the Indian Mission, I went to the hotel for my rendezvous with Bharat and Gita. The delegation left for the Beijing Planning Exhibition Hall. Let me share something about this place.

Beijing Planning Hall Exhibition

The Beijing Planning Hall Exhibition is an urban planning museum at Qianmen E Street adjacent to the Tiananmen Square. The complex has 16,000 square metres of space with half of it serving as an exhibition area.

The Hall was opened to the public on September 2004 and features a scale model of the entire layout of the Beijing metropolitan area exactly as it was in 2010. There are multimedia exhibits on history, current situation, and the future of urban planning in Beijing. There are many different exhibition zones showing different contents, including the transition through the history of this ancient city, the planning of the Olympic stadiums, and the future blueprint of a 'green' Beijing, transportation and infrastructure modernization.

This 300-square metre model of Beijing city takes up the entire floor and is best viewed with binoculars from above. The first floor has photographs of old China traditional homes and hutongs while the second, third, and fourth floors have 3D movies, booths, etc., showcasing the best of Beijing's municipal districts and a model of a futuristic house.

Between the second and third floor is a bronze wall map representing Beijing in 1949. The heart of the city is designed above all through the establishment of city walls, and then the global pattern follows the harmony rules of the yin and the yang as well as it respects the special relationship between man and heaven. The third floor has the Ancient City Evolution Area which displays the construction history of the city spanning three thousand years.

Throughout the visit, various touchscreens, virtual books, videos and specially designed rooms make your visit to this museum a pleasant one and also highlights the techno-recreational aspects of the place.

Beijing has been grappling with unprecedented atmospheric pollution since 2013. It is interesting to see how the Beijing authorities are considering green aspects in their effort to combat pollution and environmental issues. There are also 20-minute movies of 'future Beijing.'

This is the place for anyone who is curious about Beijing's past, present, and future. Ironically, for foreigners visiting the country, it is not easy to get all information about China because of stringent restrictions on the use of outside social platforms.

The Great Digital Fire Wall of China

China has its own strict social media network policy. Popular social media platforms, digital tools, apps, and sites are either banned or have restricted use. Chinese have developed their own versions of WeChat instead of WhatsApp, Baidu instead of Google, QQ instead of Facebook, Youku instead of YouTube, and so on.

I came to know during my trip that in order to popularize WeChat, the Chinese company has started a low-priced bicycle service and nearest bicycles could be located through this app. One can use a bicycle and leave it where they want to and make the payment through WeChat. Utility bills such as phone, gas, electricity, and so on can also easily be paid through WeChat.

The Chinese government controls the old and new media using monitoring systems and firewalls, shuttering publications or websites, and jailing dissident journalists, bloggers, and activists. Certain websites that the government deems potentially dangerous—such as Wikipedia, Facebook, Twitter, YouTube, and some Google services—are fully blocked or temporarily 'blacked out.' The apparatus of China's Internet control is considered more extensive and more advanced than in any other country in the world.

In China, not only do Internet platforms have to obtain a license to be able to publish content, rules have been established so Internet users are required to register and provide real-name authentication by scanning their identity cards online prior to posting anything in cyberspace.

Rather than connecting to the Internet, China has something more like an intranet within a specified boundary. China remains one of the world's most restrictive media environments. It is an irony that the Great Wall of China has its counterpart in the Great Firewall of China in the cyberspace. Thanks to the Great Firewall of China, several world-renowned Chinese artists, whose works sell in millions of dollars, do not pop up on Google search.

Meeting Chinese artists

I found Bharat and Gita waiting for me at the hotel and they introduced me to their friend, a musician Chen Qin. It was so nice of her to take a day off for a day out with us at such short notice. She was accompanying us to the meeting with a Chinese artist Du Jianghua at his residence. I was lucky to have Bharat and Gita as my interpreters since both of them were fluent in Chinese. It is very difficult to find a local artist who speaks English.

Du Jianghua is one of the most famous artists in China and a master in making clay pots. His skills, almost magical. Jianghua is the head of the Chinese Art Institution. On entering his room, I could see products of top-notch brands such as Louis Vuitton, Mont Blanc, and Gucci scattered all around. He and his wife greeted us very warmly and we all sat down at the traditional Chinese tea table. A traditional Chinese tea table has animal structures on the four corners. They are there for a good reason. When the Chinese drink tea, they keep pouring on the animal structures which is supposed to bring prosperity.

The Chinese artist and his wife were extremely courteous and it was quite interesting to be in a room full of clay teapots. The couple was extremely nice because of their relations with

Figure 2.3: With Chinese artist Du Jianghua and his wife

Bharat and Gita's musician friend. The two-and-half hour meeting was a very friendly and homely affair. I picked up a small teapot and asked the price of the teapot as per Indian currency, it was Rs 10 lakhs. I first thought there was some miscalculation, but we double-checked and it turned out to be so. I looked around, slowly seeping in the value of all the work.

Jianghua is considered to be gifted. He uses his knowledge of clay to make a wide variety of teapots. What is unique about these teapots is that its size, shape, texture, and colour are meant for serving different kinds of teas such that the tea and

Figure 2.4: With Chen Qin, Du Jianghua, and his wife (left to right)

the teapot combine to form a harmony that is supposed to have medicinal value, improves health and prevents diseases. This form of art has earned him fame and fortune.

He neither speaks nor understands English. I spoke to him and his wife via Bharat and Gita. He had heard of Mahatma Gandhi and was aware of OBOR. He presented me with a calligraphy work of my name in Chinese which he finished in my presence. He also showed me his way of making clay pots. He gifted me a small cup. I joked I could

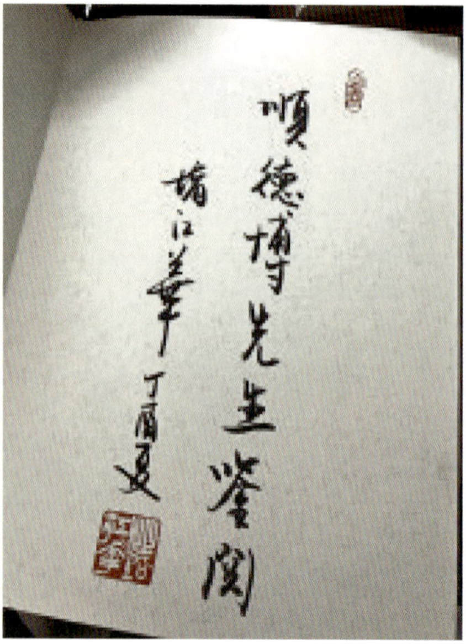

Figure 2.5: Gifted Artwork

sell it for a lot of money. He laughed and said that people who knew his work would notice his 'mark of gift' on the cup and refrain from buying it.

I was thrilled to meet an artist of such repute and learned a lot about Chinese teapots. He gave me an artwork, which he said, was a tribute to two great ancient civilizations—India and China. By the time we left, it was 7 pm.

FIGURE 2.6: Cup presented by artist Du Jianghua

Qigong

Thanks to Bharat's sincere efforts, he got us a meeting with another artist Shi Jianmin who makes contemporary paintings.

It was an hour-long drive to his studio located in the industrial zone on the outskirts of Beijing. On reaching, we saw the artist and his two friends were busy doing something that seemed like a mix of yoga and dance gestures. It is practiced worldwide for recreation, relaxation, exercise, and therapeutic effect.

Qigong (pronounced chee goong), meaning 'Life energy cultivation,' is a system of coordinated body posture and movement with rhythmic breathing and meditation. It is believed to promote health, spirituality, and martial arts training. The practice is rooted in Chinese medicine, philosophy, and martial arts. It is traditionally seen as a practice to cultivate and balance the 'chi' or 'qi' force or life energy. Like yoga, qigong is supposed to lead to higher realms of awareness.

Qigong has had its share of controversy. In 1999, in response to the widespread revival of old traditions of spirituality, morality, mysticism, and perceived challenges to state control, the Chinese government took measures to enforce control of public qigong practice, including shutting down qigong clinics and hospitals and banning groups such as Zhong Gong and Falun Gong. Since then, qigong research

Figure 2.7: With Shi Jianmin

and practice have only been officially supported in the context of health and traditional Chinese medicine.

The Chinese Health Qigong Association, established in 2000, strictly regulates public qigong practice, with the limitation of public gatherings, the requirement of state-approved training and certification of instructors, and restriction of practice to state-approved forms.

Li Hongzhi, the leader of Falun Gong is a man the Chinese government has declared a criminal. Falun Gong the spiritual movement that promotes qigong has been banned in China. Officials have arrested thousands of Falun Gong followers across China and announced plans to prosecute the movement's top leaders for subversion.

I spent an hour with them. His art collection was impressive. It was 10 pm and we started back.

Wangfujing Shopping Street

The Indian delegation was scheduled to go on a tour of Wangfujing Shopping Street. Wangfujing in Beijing is one of the most famous shopping streets in China. Since the middle of the Ming dynasty, there have been commercial activities in this place. Under the Qing dynasty, ten aristocratic estates and princess residences were built here.

Wangfujing has upscale shopping malls and the street is a shopper's delight selling paintings and traditional Chinese arts and crafts. Another Wangfujing landmark is the Foreign Languages Bookstore selling books, art supplies, videos, and CDs on several floors. The street level is the place to buy coffee table books about China in a variety of languages as well as cookbooks and books to help you learn the Chinese language.

The pedestrian mall is always buzzing with activity, especially during the warm months when sidewalk cafes flourish. Exhibitions frequently take place in the centre, especially in front of the Beijing Department Store. Toward the northern end of the mall is a large bronze statue of an old-fashioned Chinese man pulling an empty rickshaw. People line up to climb into the rickshaw to have their pictures taken by family and friends.

At the northern end of the pedestrian mall is the huge St Joseph's Cathedral, a Catholic church that was built several centuries ago by Portuguese Jesuits. The cathedral itself is open only for masses, but its courtyard makes a pleasant place to sit and relax after the hustle and bustle of walking up the mall. Chinese couples, wearing traditional Western wedding clothes, flock here on Sundays to have their wedding pictures taken.

I was feeling rather embarrassed for involving Bharat and Gita and taking up so much of their time. Bharat had fixed up dinner at an Indian restaurant at 10 pm. The restaurant is owned by Mehernosh Hoshang Pastakia. He is also the head of the Indian Association in Beijing. We thought we would reach by 10 pm but we were late. Bharat had a word with Pastakia and he said he would wait for us. When we reached the Taj Pavilion it was 11.15 pm. Pastakia treated us with a delightful Indian meal. Pastakia, a Parsi by faith, and his better half Zheng Xiowen, whom he married in 1997, oversee three restaurants in Beijing. He had first opened Taj Pavilion in 1998. He opened the second Pavilion at the Holiday Inn Lido.

My close friend and colleague Late Shri Sunil Gangopadhyay had visited Taj Pavilion on May 11, 2011, when he was the President of Sahitya Akademi. He had talked highly about the restaurant and its service. When Late Prime Minister Atal Behari Vajpayee visited China in 2003, Pastakia's restaurant was called to arrange for the culinary requirements of the Indian delegation. Again, in 2008, when former Prime Minister Manmohan Singh visited China with a delegation, Taj Pavilion served Indian dishes.

Recently, when Prime Minister, Shri Narendra Modi visited Wuhan City on April 27, 2018, to meet Chinese

Figure 2.8: With Late Sunil Gangopadhyay

President Xi Jinping, the Chinese government arranged for his stay at the Wanda Reign Wuhan Hotel which many describe as the first seven-star Hotel of China. The Hotel's general manager, Sam Chin, and his culinary team invited chefs from Taj Pavilion, Beijing, to craft cuisines for Indian Prime Minister and his delegation.

In a way Pastakia has the enviable record of serving three prime ministers of India. Pastakia informed that Narendra Modi had visited his restaurant in 2006 when he was the Chief Minister of Gujarat. Also, Late president APJ Abdul Kalam had also visited his restaurant Taj Pavilion.

While having dinner with Pastakia, I got to know about the Indian community in Beijing. There are between 600 to 800 people of Indian origin in Beijing. Apart from that, there are about 200 to 300 medical students who have come under different exchange programs. There is an Indian organization called Indian Community in Beijing (ICB). They meet once in a month, celebrate Diwali, organize *dandiya* and recently they have also started organizing the Indian Bazaar.

I found that Aamir Khan and his films are very popular in China. In fact, one taxi driver had asked me in his very broken English about *Dangal*. The Mandarin-speaking country is so crazy about Aamir Khan that *Dangal* broke all the records at the Chinese box office for any Indian film.

The Chinese love affair with Aamir Khan films began with the roaring success of *3 Idiots* and later followed by *Dhoom, Dangal*, and *PK*. Until then, Aamir Khan's fan base was confined to India and Indian diaspora only. Young Chinese viewers in millions, who saw themselves and their lives reflected in Aamir Khan's character Rancho in *3 Idiots,* became his fan overnight. The film became a cult hit to become China's 12th favourite film of all time. Only one Chinese film *Farewell My Concubine* has ranked higher.

Chinese Premier Li Keqiang during his trip to India in 2013 had his Indian interlocutors in splits when he told them how he had loved watching *3 Idiots.* The Chinese leader had then said that his daughter was so impressed with the movie that she made him watch it.

Pastakia had also told me that there was a time when Jitendra was very popular in China. Jitendra only came to know about it when he visited China and was surprised that people recognized him instantly. However, the first Indian to seep through the bamboo curtain was Raj Kapoor and his film *Awara* in the 1950s, much before Hollywood had seized a star spangled-hold of Chinese film market.

Pastakia did his hotel management in Mumbai and then opened an Indian restaurant called Omar Khayyam which flourished for 10 years before folding up in 2001. He has three branches of Taj Pavilion in Beijing. Taj Pavilion's chefs are Indian but the waitresses are young Chinese women dressed in *salwar kameez*. Taj Pavilion has been winning hearts and minds through stomachs among the Indian expatriates and young Chinese.

I was touched when he told me that though he travelled to India only once a year, his soul would always be in India.

Figure 2.9: With MH Pastakia

I liked the food in the restaurant and inquired about the spices and ingredients. He said, because of restrictions, he imported spices once a year and the rest he procures from local suppliers who route it via Hong Kong.

Talking about the Indian restaurants, I got to know about the other Indian restaurants in Beijing—Indian Kitchen, Tandoor, Raj, Mirch Masala, Ganges, Punjab, etc. It was well past midnight as we drove back to the hotel. Bharat and Gita told me they had started a Tagore India Art Restaurant in 2015–16 at the Art Centre of the city. They had kept quite a lot of artwork in and around the tables. They had run it for a year but had to close it as they did not have anyone to run it.

I felt happy about meeting Pastakia. However, when I bid adieu to Bharat and Gita, I felt as if I was parting from people I had known for eons. I wish we had more Bharats and Gitas among us. They are the true ambassadors of Indian culture and hospitality epitomizing the age-old Indian maxim from the Taittiriya Upanishad—*Atithi Devo Bhava.*

DAY 3

(24 May 2017)

The itinerary fixed by our host on the third day of our visit was quite demanding. We checked out of the hotel just before 10 am after breakfast at *The Cafe* and departed for a tour of the Great Wall of China. From there we were scheduled to reach the airport for our flight to Xi'an in the evening. The lunch was planned at the airport.

Some of the members of our delegation wanted to go back to the hotel after visiting the Great Wall and from there to the airport. I told them that the Chinese style of working was fixed. They always planned in advance and stuck to it. Predictably, when some of the members put forth this request, the Chinese officials were taken aback. They, however, checked with their seniors and apologized with a regret saying that all logistics were planned in advance. So, we checked out at half-past-nine in the morning and went for the Great Wall of China.

'He who has not climbed the Great Wall is not a true man,' said Mao Zedong. I decided not to climb as I had done so before. Instead, I waited downstairs and cleared up some office work. I was also on the lookout for Indian restaurants and Indian community members in Xi'an. Since Google was out of bounds, I thought of asking some of my contacts to help me.

The Great Wall of China

How to handle the nomads of Mongolia? For almost 2,000 years, this was the most important foreign policy question for China's rulers. The answer was Cheng Chen or the Great Wall of China.

The Great Wall is an architectural and engineering marvel of the world that was built over 27 centuries involving more than 20 dynasties of China. It stretches 21,200 kilometres across pasture lands, mountains, rivers, plateaus and deserts. The average height of the Wall is 6–7 metres with the tallest part reaching 14 metres. As of now, nearly one-fifth of the Wall is said to have been either lost or are in ruins. However, newer ones have been discovered in recent times.

Some 2,700 years ago the first sections of the Great Wall were built to keep outsiders out. Ironically, it is now being rebuilt to draw tourists in. A most massive barrier, it involves difficult engineering work and has a very long history. It is a UNESCO World Heritage Site. Watch towers and beacon towers were built high for observation and communication through signal fire. The Great Wall winds its way westward over the vast territory of China from the bank of the Yalu River and ends at the foot of snow-covered Qilianshan and Tianshan (mountains). Nearly 526 kilometres of the Wall lies in Beijing.

The work for most of the Great Wall as we see today was done under the Ming dynasty (1368–1644). Under the Ming dynasty, the Great Wall was constructed for 200 years and covered a length of 8,800 kilometres approximately. In the Qin Dynasty, the First Emperor of Qin linked the northern walls to prevent invasion from northern nations. In the Han Dynasty, the emperors extended the Great Wall far into today's western China to protect the Silk Road trade.

At different times and several different places from the 3rd century BC to the 20th century AD, they used walls to defend themselves from the nomads. The wall thus came to symbolize the social, economic, military, political, and cultural clash between China and Mongolia. Nevertheless, powerful Chinese emperors sometimes forced the nomads to submit, while at other times, as under Genghis Khan, the Mongols broke through all barriers and founded dynasties to rule China.

The Great Wall is the building project with the longest duration and greatest cost in human lives, blood, sweat and tears. Families were separated, and many workers died and were interred as part of the Great Wall itself. Contrary to the popular belief that The Great Wall is the only man-made structure visible from the moon, it can hardly be seen from the lower earth orbit.

Everyone thoroughly enjoyed the trip to the Great Wall of China. After a group photo with the Great Wall on the backdrop, we had some potato chips and coke and left for the airport. We reached the airport before the scheduled time. Our flight to Xi'an was slightly delayed. The lunch at the airport was elaborate, but I could not find anything much to eat. Not even pizzas and french fries. I did not want to embarrass our hosts who made arrangements and even told us to have our pick from any of the eateries. There were many exotic eateries, but not much on offer for a vegetarian like myself, except for cheese and fruits.

So many times during my foreign visits I have experienced that a vegetarian's choice is very limited. My problem is further compounded by my preference for Indian food. Our grandparents taught us the virtue of 'simple living and high thinking.' However, how can one think 'high' in situations where simple food habits can make you starve.

Xi'an

It was almost eight o'clock in the evening when we arrived in Xi'an city and was scheduled to check in at the Grand New Century Hotel on 333, You Yi Dong Road. A dinner was hosted for us in the restaurant at the airport.

Apart from the restaurants at Xi'an airport arrival hall, all others were about to close. I was lucky to get some french fries and when I picked up a bread bun, the interpreter told me it had meat pieces in it. On my way to the Hotel from the airport, I called up two Indian restaurants *Ganges* and *Delhi Darbar*. Both told me that they would be closed by the time I checked into the hotel.

I knew my three-day-old homemade *paranthas* were still eatable and would see me through the night. However, I got a call on my Chinese number from Gyan, manager of the *Ganges* Indian restaurant. He learned from me that I was with a delegation. He had offered to bring *dal-chawal* for me to my Hotel on his way back and requested me to instruct the front desk of the Hotel accordingly. I took out my small diary where I had written down the contact number of the hotel. I have this habit of writing down all the numbers that I might need during my travels.

The hotel answered my call, but I had quite a time trying to explain to the voice on the other end to pay for the Indian food which I would square-up on reaching the hotel. I had almost given up in vain and was about to call up Gyan, when the interpreter, who had overheard my conversation, called up the hotel and explained the whole thing. Language remains a major barrier in China. Very few people speak English, even in big hotels. Though Xi'an is a major International tourist destination famed for its Terracotta Warriors, yet the top starred hotels of the city lack English-speaking staff.

By the time we reached the hotel, it was half past ten. There were very few senior staff on duty. The hotel staff—from the bell-boys to the receptionist to the room service personnel—everyone carried a phone-like device with a speaker into which they spoke in Chinese which was translated into English. The device made one-way rudimentary communication possible since it could not translate English into Chinese.

Members of our delegation tried their best to ask the staff for drinking water and also inquire if the tap water was potable. However, neither the staff nor the device could understand. I called a bell-boy and using hand gestures asked him to accompany me to the bar and showed him a bottle of water. He nodded. Soon enough, he came back with a bottle of scotch, glasses and ice.

I realized there was a bottle of scotch next to the water bottle. Again, I returned to the bar with him and showed him the water bottle by going behind the bar counter. I took no chances, picked up the water bottle and came out. I was really upset thinking that this popular hotel may not be getting enough international tourists.

The *dal-chawal* was god-sent. Though no longer warm, not a drop or a grain was left by the time I cleared my plate. Indian food and water at the end of the day. *'Ant bhala to sab bhala' (all is well that ends well).*

One thing that became very clear during my visit to China was the muted admiration for Prime Minister Narendra Modi among the Chinese officials. Much of it was couched in diplomatic niceties but there were moments I could sense that Modi was a keenly observed subject of deep research among the Chinese think tanks and policymakers. One of the reasons could be that Modi has met Chinese President Xi Jinping 13 times in the past five years.

The prestigious CIIS published a paper acknowledging India's diplomacy under Modi as vibrant and assertive. CIIS, where we had our meetings with Chinese counterparts, has described this distinctive and unique diplomacy in a paper called 'Modi Doctrine,' which, I think, is an incisive report on Modi's successful diplomatic achievements which aptly sums up Modi's vision of a 'New India' by 2022.

Modi doctrine

Modi had surprised the Chinese mandarins during his trip to Wuhan in Hubei province with a revelation. The Chinese had made elaborate arrangements for Modi. He was served Assam tea instead of Chinese tea and the tablecloths laid were brought from Gujarat. Modi's humble origin and his career from being a tea seller to the prime minister of India are known to many Chinese. The Chinese usually are meticulous in their approach and do their homework well in advance.

During his first one-on-one meeting with President Xi at the Hubei Provincial Museum, Modi told his host that this was his second visit to Hubei province, surprising the Chinese officials, who otherwise keep a track of all bilateral and official visits minutely. Chinese ambassador to India, Luo Zhaohui, had revealed to the Indian media later, 'We didn't know that Prime Minister Modi had visited Wuhan earlier.'

Modi told Xi that when he was the Gujarat chief minister, he had an opportunity to visit central China's Hubei Province on a study tour to learn about the massive Three Gorges Dam. 'The speed with which you constructed this dam and its scale inspired me. So, I came on a study tour and spent a day at the dam,' Modi had told Xi. The Three Gorges project is the world's largest hydroelectric power project. It is a multi-functional water control system on the mighty Yangtze river comprising a dam stretching over 2 kilometres and 185 metres high. It has 32 hydro-powered turbo-generators and a five-tier ship lock and ship lift system.

There are many such anecdotes that have made Modi popular among the Chinese. The Chinese officials feel that fully understanding the characteristics and trends of the 'Modi Doctrine' will be of great practical significance in maintaining the healthy and stable development in China-India relations in the long run. After all, the combined population of China-India is over two-and-half billion, which means a huge market with immense potential.

The basic observation put forth by the Chinese think tank in 'Modi Doctrine' is that Prime Minister Modi has inherited and further developed a major power diplomatic strategy for India since the end of the Cold War reflecting Modi's personal political philosophy and style of administration.

Modi gave a clear message when he undertook his first visit as the Prime Minister of India to the smallest nation in South Asia—Bhutan. Modi took concrete steps to exchange enclaves with Bangladesh and remove the long-standing discord between the two countries. India and Bangladesh relations are at an all-time high.

The Chinese establishment also sees Modi's South Asia diplomacy as an attempt to increase its control over smaller neighbours and scuttle the presence or growing influence in the region of other forces outside South Asia. The paper says South Asia policy under the 'Modi Doctrine' focuses on tightening the bond between India and neighbouring countries, and better serving India's economic and social development strategy by promoting regional and sub-regional connectivity.

In recent years, India has accelerated cooperation mechanisms such as the Bay of Bengal Initiative for multi-sectoral cooperation and the 'Bhutan-Bangladesh-India-Nepal Connectivity Cooperation,' with a view towards forging an India-led regional and sub-regional cooperation framework. The concept and practice of the 'Modi Doctrine' reflected in South Asia diplomacy, when compared to previous administrations, has highlighted both its own authority as well as the benefits it can provide to its neighbours, and is more concerned about its dominance in South Asia.

The Chinese see that South Asia is one area where Indian and Chinese interests can clash. Another factor mentioned in the 'Modi Doctrine' is the strengthening of common interests in the larger periphery. Since its launch of the Look East policy in 1992, India has expended much talk but little action, and in its relations with its ASEAN partners, India has failed to play a major role. After taking office in 2014, Modi proposed the strategy of Act East, emphasizing practical actions to enhance relations with ASEAN. After that, high-level exchanges between India and the ASEAN countries have been frequent, and India continues to voice its opinion on issues of concern to ASEAN.

India has identified ASEAN as the guest of honour during the 2018 'Republican Day' celebration. The ten leaders of ASEAN members visited India. One of the priorities of India's Act East is infrastructure connectivity, that is, accelerating the construction of transport corridors connecting the east and west, promoting road construction in the northeastern region, and removing the 'bottlenecks' hindering connectivity within ASEAN.

With the aid of Japan and other countries, the Indian section of the 'Kaladan Multi-Modal Transit Transport (KMMTT)' linking Kolkata to the Sittwe Port of Myanmar has been fully launched. The India-Myanmar-Thailand highway project has been advanced at a faster pace. After Modi took office, India's neighbourhood strategy has accelerated markedly. He emphasized that India's interest should no longer be confined to the South Asian subcontinent, but should be extended to a vast area from the Gulf of Aden to Malacca.

India's 'Neighborhood First' strategy has quickly pushed the country westward to Middle East and Africa. For over three years, Modi has not only visited major countries in the region such as Saudi Arabia, the United Arab Emirates, Qatar and Iran, but he has also become India's first Prime Minister to visit Israel.

India has also opened up strategic channels to Afghanistan and Central Asia, and tightened its political and economic relations with the Gulf countries in the Middle East via Iran. It is true that his proactive moves in the Middle East are also aimed at isolating Pakistan diplomatically, but more importantly, Modi seeks to better safeguard India's strategic interests such as energy security in the Gulf region, thus serving the long-term need for the country to be a great power. Modi government has accelerated its promotion of an Indian Ocean strategy and proposed the five-pronged strategy on the Indian Ocean. India proclaims itself to be the 'net security provider' in the Indian Ocean region.

For a long time, India had adopted a rather vigilant and exclusionist attitude toward any incursion of other major powers into the Indian Ocean. Since Modi took office, India has adjusted its policy to put more emphasis on the strategic cooperation and coordination with the US, Japan and other countries, taking advantage of the power of the US and Japan in an attempt to maintain its own advantageous position in the competition among the major powers in the Indo-Pacific region.

In 2015, the military exercise in Malabar between the US and India extended an invitation to Japan to participate. When Modi visited the United States in June 2016, he clearly demonstrated the strategic significance of bilateral cooperation in the Indo-Pacific region. India's strategic sector responded positively to the initiative of the United States and Japan to construct an 'Indo-Pacific Alliance'.

US-India strategic cooperation is a big move. India-US cooperation in defence and security has been further strengthened. The United States promised to help India build its aircraft carrier and transfer anti-submarine technology to India. The two countries also signed an agreement on logistics support, which further enriched their strategic cooperation, especially defence cooperation.

After Trump came to power, India was initially quite sceptical about the trend of US domestic and foreign policies.

Modi was concerned that Trump's 'America First' policy would undermine the momentum of India-US relations.

In June 2017, after Modi's visit to the United States, US-India bilateral relations continued on a stable footing. At the same time, India has also begun to actively expand its relations with the EU. India continues to maintain its traditional relations with Russia and has attached great importance to strengthening cooperation and coordination with emerging powers.

India has actively promoted the trilateral dialogue among China, Russia, and India, striven to become a member of the Shanghai Cooperation Organization, paid more attention to its strategic investment in the BRICS (Brazil Russia India China South Africa) cooperation mechanism, and actively participated in such mechanisms as the Asian Infrastructure Investment Bank and the New Development Bank.

India plays its role among the major powers such as the US and Russia and strives to achieve benefits on all sides. Such an approach has not only maximized its political security and economic interests but more importantly, has maintained and strengthened its initiative in the interaction at the strategic level among the major powers.

After taking office, Modi surprisingly adjusted the Indian position on global issues such as climate change, the Doha round of WTO negotiations and sustainable development. India has actively participated in the negotiations while overcoming domestic difficulties and has played an important role in the conclusion of the Paris Accord.

Modi's strong and decisive governing style and pragmatic governance philosophy began to affect the diplomatic field. While insisting on advancing all-round diplomacy, Modi has adopted a 'coalition not alliance' strategy on many major regional and international issues so as to increase India's bargaining chips in the great power games.

Modi has stressed that India should strive to maintain its strategic independence while playing a role among major powers. India will not become a vassal of any other country and will not rely on security guarantees from others.

New Issues for 'Modi Doctrine': The 'Modi Doctrine' is the product of India's rapid economic growth and the consequent increase of its overall national strength over the past 20 years. As an emerging power, India has been supported in recent years by the international community, especially the United States and other Western countries.

This has not only enhanced India's international status but also bolstered India's sense of being a major power; self-confidence has soared to an all-time high. The 'Modi Doctrine' serves India's rise to a leading power.

Modi Doctrine on Sino-India relations: Since Modi took office, the development of overall relations between China and India has maintained steady momentum. Both leaders attach great importance to bilateral relations. However, with the rise of competitive factors in recent years, and the increasing challenges and complexity at the global, regional and bilateral levels, a situation has developed in which new problems keep emerging while old ones remain.

The Doklam incident not only highlighted the border issue but also for a time seemed to imperil the overall relationship between the two countries. The complicated changes in China-India relations in recent years are largely due to the readjustment of international structure. India also believes that it should continue to strengthen its strategic relations with the United States and Japan in order to seek a stronger position in dealing with China.

For the Chinese academia, what concerns them most is India's strategic orientation toward China, in particular, they are wary of India's defence and security cooperation with the United States and Japan. Modi continues to see China as Pakistan's all-weather friend, which is a big stumbling block toward improving Sino-Indian ties.

DAY 4

(25 May 2017)

The breakfast at the Grand New Century Hotel was a grand affair. It was a lavish spread that would hands-down beat any international luxury five-star hotel. Though, I had to make do good with cornflakes, milk and toast only. The Grand New Century Hotel Xi'an is situated close to the Xi'an Museum, Small Goose Pagoda (Xiaoyanta), Big Wild Goose Pagoda (Dayanta) and the Lianhu Ancient City Wall.

We left the Hotel around 9 am for a tour of the Xi'an City Wall from the southern gate. First, let me share some facts about Xi'an City which is the capital of Shaanxi Province.

Xi'an City

Xi'an, which means 'Western Peace,' is the capital of Shaanxi Province of China. The name was adopted in 1369 under the early Ming dynasty. Xi'an is one of the oldest cities in China and the oldest of the four ancient capitals. Xi'an became a cultural and political centre of China in the 11th century BC with the founding of the Zhou dynasty.

Figure 4.1: Author at the New Century

Xi'an is located at the centre of Guanzhong Plain in Northwestern China and is the starting point of the Silk Road. It is home to the famous Terracotta Army of Emperor Qin Shi Huang. The present-day Xi'an has been the site of several important former Chinese cities. The Wei river provides the city with potable water.

Shaanxi Province is one of the 23 provinces of China. The People's Republic of China considers Taiwan as its 24th province which is the source of all its disputes with Chinese Taipei. Besides provinces, China has four municipalities—Beijing, Tianjin, Shanghai and Chongqing; five autonomous regions Guangxi, Inner Mongolia, Tibet, Ningxia, Xinjiang, and two Special Administrative Regions—Hong Kong and Macau. In all, there are 34 provincial-level administrative units.

With a 12 million population, Xi'an is a sub-provincial city. Since 1990, the city has re-emerged as an important cultural, industrial and educational hub with facilities for research and development, software and China's space exploration program. It was reported by *The Economist* to be one of China's 13 emerging megapolises.

Some of the landmarks of Xi'an City are Xi'an Terracotta Warriors Museum, Giant Wild Goose Pagoda, Drum Tower of Xi'an, Bell Tower of Xi'an, City Wall of Xi'an, Tang Paradise and others. A large number of historical monuments, ancient ruins, city walls, mausoleums, temples, tombs and pagodas have made Xi'an a popular International tourist destination.

In October 1911, during the revolution in which the Qing dynasty was overthrown, revolutionary forces massacred 20,000 Manchus in the northeastern zone within Xi'an's city walls, wiping out the entire Manchu population in the city.

In 1936, the Xi'an Incident took place inside the city during the Chinese Civil War. The incident brought the Kuomintang (KMT) and the Communist Party of China to a truce in order to concentrate on fighting against the Japanese

Invasion. On 20 May 1949, the Communist-controlled People's Liberation Army captured the city of Xi'an from the Kuomintang forces.

A bicycle-sharing network started operating in 2013 and today has 52,000 bikes, used by over 2,00,000 people every day.

Xi'an City Wall: For a city with a history stretching over two millenniums with its famous 2,000-year-old Terracotta Warriors, the 637-year-old Xi'an City Wall is a relatively new kid on the block. The Wall is a rigorous and integrated military defence system comprising city moat, drawbridge, various observation towers, battlements, turrets, parapets, and crenels.

At 40 feet high and 45 feet wide, the 14-kilometre-long Xi'an City Wall is the most complete ancient city wall in China. It offers a magnificent panoramic of China's most fascinating city and its ancient-urban continuity.

This ancient structure is the only fortification in China that still stands as an unbroken rectangular circuit that represents one of the oldest, largest and best-preserved Chinese City Walls. A 20-feet deep moat runs around the Wall. This made it necessary to have drawbridges.

When Zhu Yuanzhang, the first Emperor of the Ming Dynasty (1368–1644), captured Huizhou, heeding the advise of a hermit named Zhu Sheng, 'built high walls, store abundant food supplies and take time to be an Emperor,' he started to fortify the city as a military defense system and unify the other states.

After the establishment of the Ming dynasty, Zhu began to enlarge the wall built initially during the old Tang Dynasty (618–907 AD), forming today's scale of Xian City Wall. There are 98 ramparts which were built to defend against the enemy from climbing up. Each rampart has a sentry building, in which the soldiers could protect the entire wall without exposing themselves to the enemy.

Since the weapons in those days did not have the power to break through a wall, the enemies attacked the gates to enter the city. Thus, complicated gate structures were built within the wall. The Wall was once one of the most impressive military defense systems in the world. Nearly 13 Chinese dynasties had Xi'an as their capital.

The Wall includes four gates called Changle (eternal joy) in the east, Anding (harmony peace) in the west, Yongning (eternal peace) in the south and Anyuan (forever harmony) in the north. The South Gate akaYongning is the most time-honoured, magnificent and beautifully decorated of all city gates located near the Bell Tower at the centre of the city. Built in 582 AD (Sui Dynasty), the gate is among the oldest gates of the Xi'an Ancient City Wall. As one of the three southern gates close to the east, it was originally named after Anshang Gate. It was designated Main South Gate at the end of the Tang Dynasty. It finally got the current name 'Yongning Gate' during the Ming Dynasty. Government ceremonies are usually held in this South Gate Square.

The South Gate Square was restored and formally opened to the public in September 2014. Covering a U-shaped area of around 32,000 square meters, the square is divided into three parts, main royal road, secondary royal road and celebration square. There is a large underground parking lot below it. Tourists can enjoy a free visit to two museums inside the Barbican and the archery tower of the South Gate. Eighteen gates encircle the rectangle-shaped city centre of Xi'an, but not all are open for visitors. Visitors can ascend the Wall from the South Gate, Small South Gate, East Gate, West Gate, North Gate, Heping Gate, Wenchang Gate, and Hanguang Gate.

You can choose the nearest city gate according to your location. No matter which gate you choose, you can tour the whole circle of the wall if you like. It has been refurbished many times since it was built in the 14th century, thrice at intervals of about 200 years in the latter half of the 1500s and 1700s. In 1983, it got a major facelift to form the closed-circuit network that exists now.

Along the top of the wall is a walkway, which would typically take four hours to cover. Bicycling along the 14-kilometre long City Wall is popular with the tourists. Outside the Wall are the high rises, billboards, highways, plazas and swanky cars that flaunt the wealth of the nouveau riche.

The Xi'an City Wall is on the tentative list of UNESCO World Heritage Site under the title 'City Walls of the Ming and Qing Dynasties.' Since 2008, it is also on the list of the State Administration of Cultural Heritage of China. Since March 1961, the Xi'an City Wall is a heritage National Historical and Cultural Unit.

The Xi'an City Wall has survived countless wars over centuries. It came close to being demolished during the 1950s when other historic city walls in Beijing and Hangzhou were felled. The reason for this was that city walls were considered a feudal legacy that stood in the way of social advances promised by the Great Leap Forward.

The Xi'an Wall owes its survival to a renowned historian who opposed the wall's destruction and successfully lobbied with the then Secretary-General of the Council, Xi Zhongxun, father of current Chinese President Xi Jinping, to spare the wall.

After our visit to the South Gate Wall, it was a part of our itinerary to visit Muslim Street in Xi'an.

Muslim Street: As the name implies, the Muslim Street or Muslim Quarter is the hub of the Chinese Muslim community of Xi'an. It is located to the north of the West Street in the city centre, the Quarter covers several blocks inhabited by 20,000 to 30,000 Muslims. There are nine mosques, including smaller ones in the area, of which, the Great Mosque in the Huajue Lane is the most famous and popular.

Muslim food and souvenir market is another feature of the area. The Beiyuanmen Muslim Market located just to the north of the Drum Tower is a great choice after sightseeing in the city centre. Xi'an was the first city in China to be introduced to Islam. Emperor Gaozong of the Tang dynasty officially allowed the practice of Islam in AD 651. Xi'an has a large Muslim community, the significant majority is from the Hui group, there are an estimated 50,000 Hui Muslims in Xi'an. There are seven major mosques in Xi'an; the best known is the Great Mosque as mentioned.

The main food street area is known as Huimin Street. It is the main street with a few intersecting roads. So the Xi'an Muslim Food Street is the collective name for a number of streets, including Beiyuanmen Street, North Guangji Street, Xiyangshi Street and Dapiyuan Street, and it has become a famous attraction of Xi'an for Muslim cultural ambience. I must caution vegetarians that Muslim Street is a haven for meat lovers, and there is meat all around.

Xi'an was the starting point of the ancient Silk Road about a thousand years ago during the Western Han Dynasty (206 BC–9 AD). A number of merchants from Arabia and Persia went to Xi'an for business; they settled down there what is at present called the Muslim Street. The locals called them the Hui people.

A number of ancient architectural buildings are well retained on the street. Hanguang Gate of the Tang dynasty (618–907), Xicheng Gate Tower Cluster of the Ming dynasty (1368–1644), the City God Temple (a Taoist temple) and the Grand Mosque, all of which contrast finely with one another.

The Great Mosque of Xi'an is the biggest in the province and is also known as the Huajue Mosque as it is located on the street by the same name. Much of the mosque was built during the Hongwu reign of early Ming dynasty and currently houses 20 buildings in its five courtyards spread over one 130,000 square feet.

In 1956, the mosque was declared a Historical and Cultural Site Protected at the Shaanxi Province level. Later it was declared a Major Historical and Cultural Site Protected at the National Level in 1988. The mosque is still used as a place of worship by Chinese Muslims or Hui people.

While tourists consider Muslim Street a scenic spot, the locals see it as a snack street. Unending series of eateries and food stalls make it a food street selling cakes, dried fruit or bread, barbecued meats on skewers. You would also see folks making candy. There are also fruit pies made with persimmon here which are considered unique refreshment in Xi'an.

Among the famous must-try dishes of Xi'an at the Muslim Street are, *roujiamo*—marinated beef or lamb stuffed inside a freshly baked bun; another traditional Uighur dish is the *yangrou paomo*—pita bread soaked in lamb soup. You can find a variety of soups here with all kinds of meats in them, including sheep blood. Xi'an dumplings also come in the form of bean threads in Shaanxi flavoring. Xi'an is also known for its cold noodles made from rice or flour. There are dozens of noodle stalls offering it.

Beiyuanmen Muslim Street has a long history. It is said that in olden days, foreign diplomatic envoys and merchants lived here and then they married and had children. Today, most of the inhabitants here are the descendants of those immigrants.

The Muslims of Xi'an is a closely knit community, which maintains its own culture and traditions to this day. Walking along this twisted, narrow street, which is aligned with stores on both sides, you can see that Muslim men with white hats and white beards sit inside the stores as children run around playing.

After the visit to the Muslim Street, there was a lunch scheduled at 11.30 am at the Tialongbaoyan Restaurant. A first glance at the restaurant confirmed its grandeur. It was a fancy vegetarian restaurant. Again, the vegetarian food tasted like non-vegetarian stuff. The Chinese officials had booked a private room for us in this restaurant. I got to eat some Chinese rice and spicy curry and huge pieces of watermelon. The curry, though made of vegetarian ingredients, was named after a fish dish. This restaurant is quite popular because of its private dining rooms.

After lunch, we headed for the Museum of Terracotta Warriors and Horses. The Terracotta Warriors is perhaps only second to the Great Wall of China in popularity. It leaves you awestruck.

Terracotta Warriors of Xi'an

In March 1974 a farmer called Yang Xinman and his co-workers were the first to discover the Terracotta Army while digging a well not far from the First Emperor Qin's tomb. After Yang's spade struck one of the terracotta warrior's head they tried to move it thinking it to be a rock.

Yang and his workers reported their chance discovery to the authorities little realizing that it would go on to become one of the greatest archaeological excavations of the century. Four Terracotta Army pits about 25 feet deep were unearthed. One of the pits was empty which lead experts to believe that the work could not be completed during Emperor Qin Shihuang's lifetime.

The life-sized terracotta figures are seemingly different from each other just like the soldiers in any real army. Their faces, physique, facial expressions, height, and poise are different. Same with their uniforms. The rank and file of the terracotta warriors are well defined and includes foot soldiers, cavalrymen, archers, generals and so on. About a dozen basic face shapes have been identified.

The much-excavated 750 by 200 feet wide first pit contains over 8,000 figures and was perhaps the abode of the main army. The second pit, partially excavated, reveals chariots, horses and cavalrymen. The crescent-shaped third pit is fully excavated and is relatively smaller than the others. It has one main chariot that occupies the centre and 68 high-ranking warriors. Archaeologists consider this pit represents the command centre. The fourth pit is empty and signifies that the work came to a stop or could not be completed.

New findings through the use of technology has revealed that the Terracotta Army is a representation of Emperor Qin's army and Imperial Palace.

These Terracotta findings have recently made news in the Indian newspapers as well when Prime Minister Narendra Modi visited it during his trip to China. With a little luck, a visitor of Terracotta Army may run into one of the three

Figure 4.2: Terracotta Warrior Museum

men who discovered it and even get an autographed copy of the official guidebook.

To know a bit about this grand archaeological wonder, one has to delve into China's past and its First Emperor Qin Shihuang. The First Emperor Qin is an important figure in Chinese history. At the age of 13, he became King of Qin (chin) state. Over the next 25 years, established the Qin Empire in 221 BCE by defeating many smaller warring states. 'Qin' is thought to be the origin of the modern English word 'China.' He ruled as the First Emperor from 221–210 BCE.

The Qin dynasty was located in the heart of the Yellow River Valley in Shaanxi. During Qin Shihuang's reign, the Qin capital was Xianyang, near Xi'an. Xianyang was a majestic capital covering more than 45 square kilometres.

The importance of Qin in China's long history is indelible as he is considered to be the First Emperor of China. His military expansion created a unified China, with a centralized government, for the first time in history. In his capital, Xianyang, close to Xi'an, he built hundreds of palaces, the likes of which had not been seen before in China. The First Emperor standardized systems of law, weights and measurements, writing, and currency.

He connected walls, built by previous rulers, to form the Great Wall of China as a barrier to enemies. He directed the construction of his own burial complex, now known as one of the greatest Chinese archaeological discoveries.

Emperor Qin wanted to accomplish a feat that would leave his mark on history for generations to come. He ordered his workers to carry out a gargantuan project to construct an underground Spirit Army as a part of his Imperial complex. He wanted it to look as real as possible. With no reference point, the workers and artisans had to start from scratch. Collecting ideas and techniques and gathering knowledge of processes and procuring materials from regions near and far.

The artisans followed some basic rules. In order to give stability to the figures, they made the base of the figures heavier and the upper portions, in contrast, were hollow. Single or multiple moulds were used to give shape to the figures. Hair,

Figure 4.3: Sundeep Bhutoria at the Terracotta Warrior Museum

caps, and helmets were added separately. Beards, eyebrows, and moustaches were added separately to each figure a unique look. The uniforms matched that of the real army and army insignias were used for effect.

Dinner

From the museum we went to the hotel, an official dinner hosted by the Foreign Affairs Office of Shaanxi Province at

5.30 pm at the same hotel. By the time we reached the hotel, there was still some time for dinner. Dikanchi D Shira and I decided to walk to a nearby mall.

While having a chat with her over coffee I came to know that although she is a Member of the Legislative Assembly, it was by chance she came into politics. Her husband, the Chief Minister of Meghalaya, and the party had requested her to contest the seat. She won easily and is now committed to her constituency and the people.

The evening sit-down dinner was in the same hotel and the Deputy Foreign Minister, Gong Guijun of Foreign Affairs

Figure 4.4: Author with Ms Dikanchi D Shira and Gong Guijun

Office, was our host. Gong, an amiable person, briefed us on many topics. He was in-charge of Prime Minister Narendra Modi's visit to Xi'an. He regaled us with anecdotes of Modi's visit, local medicines, and the magic belt, which is supposed to be good for the bones and so on.

I asked Gong Guijun, why Xi'an being such a popular International tourist spot had no directions in English and the hotel staff hardly spoke the English language. He smiled and said, 'Our domestic tourism is huge and we are more than happy with our home tourists.'

During the 20-course dinner, which went on till 8.30 pm, I learned much about China. Their thinking, worldview,

Figure 4.5: Author with Gong Guijun

their approach towards life and so on. After dinner, we went to the hotel bar to order coffee. We succeeded with the help of the duty manager. I was glad I attended this dinner as I had missed the dinner in Shanghai hosted by Shanghai Foreign Affairs Office.

Xinjiang—a festering wound

As I reflected on the day's visit to the Muslim Street, I realized that the apparently peaceful look could be so deceptive. China has a big problem with its ethnic Muslim minorities. When one talks of Muslims in China, the name of Xinjiang is bound to come up.

Xinjiang, originally called Xiyu or western territory, is considered to be one of the most isolated regions of China. Strategically it is among the most important provinces located 4,000 kilometres away from Beijing. Xinjiang is a Muslim majority province of China.

In many ways, Xinjiang is like Kashmir. A festering wound that has led to protests, bloodletting, terrorism, and brutal government crackdowns. The basic cause of unrest is the ethnic-Islamic identity of local Uighurs. Xiyu became Xinjiang, meaning 'new borders,' in the middle of the eighteenth century when it became a Chinese territory under the Manchu dynasty. China declared it a province in 1884 and re-named it. It is officially known as the Xinjiang Uighur Autonomous Region (XUAR).

The fact that Xinjiang shares borders with Afghanistan, India, Pakistan, Mongolia, Kazakhstan, Russia, Kyrgyzstan, and Tajikistan makes it as much important to China as Kashmir is to India. India maintains a studied silence on Xinjiang. So does China on Kashmir. Another fact is that Xinjiang falls on the BRI or 'The Silk Route' which is at the heart of China's new global economic plan. Also, the Aksai Chin region, over which India has a dispute with China, comes under XUAR.

XUAR gained much importance after abundant oil and mineral reserves were found. It is currently China's largest natural gas-producing region. During the 1950–70, the Chinese government started the state-sponsored migration of Han Chinese to Xinjiang to counter the Soviet-supported Uighurs, Uzbeks, Tajiks, Kirghiz, and Kazakh minorities who are considered to be the Turkic people. Han Chinese, Russians, Manchurians, and Indians comprise the non-Turkic group. The Uighurs, who follow Islam, are the largest group. The Uighur Muslims are Sunnis.

The Uighur separatism based on their Islamic identity was fanned by the Soviet support. Numerous camps were set up across the border inside the Soviet Union in the 1960s from where Uighurs and Kazakhs launched militant campaigns against China. The two red giants, Russia and China, had a border clash in 1969. Ten years later, when the then-Soviet Union invaded Afghanistan, China returned the favour by supporting the Afghan *mujahideen,* providing safe havens, camps and light arms and ammunition against the Soviet forces.

The Chinese government accuses Uighurs of religious separatism and has adopted a policy of suppressing their culture and Islamic identity. This lead to the alienation and radicalization of the Uighurs and a spate of riots and violent incidents with Han Chinese population has rocked China since the 1990s. Government buildings were bombed and security forces attacked and killed by Uighur separatists.

The Three Evils: The Chinese government calls religious extremism, terrorism, and separatism as the three evils. China began a clampdown in late 1995 to weed out these evils. The government sees Islam as the cause of the Uighur ethic-nationalist unrest and a threat to the state. China has imposed sweeping restraints on the Uighurs resulting in a steady erosion of social, economic and cultural rights.

Scores of incidents of bombings, rioting, and knife attacks by Uighurs left hundreds dead and thousands injured. The Chinese government changed its policy to tackle Xinjiang unrest in an unprecedented scale after the July 2009 riots.

In the meanwhile, the World Uighur Congress (WUC) was formed by a group of exiled Uighur leaders, which operates out of Munich, Germany, in 2004. This is a non-violent group, which operates as a non-governmental organization (NGO) and a human rights think tank, espousing the cause of Uighurs by highlighting the discriminatory policies of China. WUC submits parallel human rights violation reports to the United Nations.

WUC has reported that many Uighurs detained by the Chinese Government have simply disappeared without a trace. The Uighurs call for asserting their Islamic religious and cultural identity which is more Turkic than Chinese. The WUC had successfully highlighted in the Western media alleged human rights transgressions by the Chinese government, which China has denied.

The Chinese government claims that it allows freedom of religion. This is strangely true and false at the same time. This is so because China actually has a dual policy with regard to freedom of religion concerning Muslim minorities. While the Chinese have intruded into and control almost every aspect of Uighur Muslims who are *Sunni*s, the Hui Muslims (*Shiah*s) are spared. The Hui Muslims are allowed to profess their Islamic faith, build mosques, follow Muslim dietary laws and practices, wear headscarves and so on.

The Hui Muslims are mainly found in the northwest of the Chinese provinces and the Zongyuan region. According to the 2011 census, China is home to approximately 10.5 million Hui people, the majority of whom are Chinese-speaking practitioners of Islam. There are others who practice other religions.

China has gone to extreme levels to implement harsh policies to suppress Islam in Xinjiang but has allowed the

Hui ethnic group much freedom to profess their Islamic faith. Some of the Islamic countries have criticized China openly for its policies. Of late, the issue of Xinjiang has soured China's relations with Turkey.

Political re-education centres: China has put in place an extensive 'Social Management System' grid to combat radicalization of Uighurs in Xinjiang by 're-educating' them in specially set up centres. An elaborate security apparatus uses the latest technologies and spyware for surveillance. According to recent media reports, thousands of Uighurs and other Muslims in Xinjiang have disappeared into the 're-education centres' or *maktap* (internment camps), set up by the Chinese government.

Any Muslim in Xinjiang who looks too religious; has travelled abroad to study or has relatives who did so; use non-Chinese social media apps in their phones and electronic devices; who follow religious practices such as fasting; opt for halal food and so on, can be detained and taken in for re-education. The re-education centres operate more like internment camps for indoctrination where one is required to study the Chinese language, state laws on Islam and come to appreciate the Chinese Communist Party. The purpose is to stem 'extremification' within society as outlined in the XUAR Regulations on De-extremification which seeks to make religion more Chinese. WUC calls it religious and cultural cleansing.

Orwellian world: There are many stories building up around these re-education centres. Possessing a Quran, dressing in Islamic style, possessing religious books have landed many to the centres. There have been reports of torture and deaths in custody of many religious scholars. One early victim was master *dutar* player, Abdurehim Heyit, who was sentenced to 10 years imprisonment for performing a song lauding the sacrifice of Uighur ancestors, was told he would never perform live or record songs again.

Uighurs face difficulty travelling within Xinjiang and many live in fenced-off neighbourhoods with checkpoints at every point of entry. In Southern Urumqui each house has a QR code (Quick Response Code) so that the security can easily see photos of the authorized residents who reside there. Those Uighurs in Xinjiang who do not end up in the internment camps have to go through 'Becoming Family' policy of the Communist Party of China. This involves visiting of Uighur homes by Han relatives. Police can also swoop down on individuals and check the apps being used in their phones. Using non-Chinese social media network apps in a mobile phone is a punishable offence.

In 2017, tens of thousands of teams of Chinese officials arrived in Xinjiang to report extremist behavior in society. Undesirable aspects and behavior such as keeping long beards; fasting during Ramzan; insisting on halal food; keeping Qurans; wearing headscarves and so on. The locals were categorized as trustworthy, average or untrustworthy depending upon their age, employment status, religious knowledge and leanings and so on. Praying five times a day, which is a very common feature among devout Muslims, was categorized as extreme behavior. The mosques are watched closely by the government and are more or less empty during main Friday prayers.

In 2018, the Chinese government scaled up the 'Becoming Family' programme to make it mandatory for each Uighur household to have a specified number of 'home stays' by Chinese officials in their homes. During this enforced home stays, the Uighur householders are to cooperate and provide detailed information about their political views and private lives. The home stays last for a few weeks to months and may be repeated many times throughout the year.

During this enforced home-stay period, the Muslim families are introduced to cultural elements alien to them or even considered a taboo. It would be considered extreme behavior on the part of a Muslim family to ask if the Chinese dishes from the mainland prepared in their homes by their Han 'friends' contained pork.

It is a strange Orwellian world where the Big Brother comes and shares your food, sleeps in your bed and tells your children how to think and be good citizens by appreciating the benevolent Communist Party of China. The Muslim families in Xinjiang live under the watchful eyes of the officials who report their findings to the authority, which determines what kind of social life the family would have in the days ahead. Many Uighur women are reported to have opted to marry Han Chinese men in order to pre-empt their families from landing up in re-education centers.

Why did the People's Republic of China resort to such draconian measures in Xinjiang?

The answer is not easy. In 2001, China embraced the Global War on Terror (GWOT). After the 2008 Urumchi riots between locals and state police, the government began hardening its stance. After a further outbreak of violence perpetrated by militant Uighurs in Xinjiang in 2012 and 2015, the Chinese government labelled 'religious extremism' to include all religious behavior and not just violent behavior by Muslims. Thus, began a policy of religious policing and 'de-extremify' the Uighur society.

Mass indoctrination and eradication of religion-based cultural norms and practices of Uighurs seem to be the main focus. It is hoped that the next generation of Uighurs, severed from their Turkic past, would be more Chinese than their parents and grandparents.

Like the Hindu-Muslim co-existence or the *Ganga-Yamuna tehzeeb* that witnessed a rich fusion of Hindu-Muslim culture, the Uighurs and Han Chinese—who were in the minority in the 1950s—had a similar cordial friendly communal relationship. Many Han Chinese became fluent in Uighur language and took to the dietary habits and other practices that Uighurs considered *haram*. The Communist Party of China's state nationality policies were progressive from the Western perspective and allowed local religious practices and mother-tongue education of minorities.

This communal harmony came under attack during Mao's Cultural Revolution. Mosques were demolished, Red

Guards forced Muslims to raise pigs and eat pork. Islam went underground only to resurface under Deng Xiaoping's regime in the 1980s. China's hard policy approach has not entirely succeeded. One of the purposes is to ensure religious leaders do not advocate fundamentalism or radicalism as defined by the state and prevent them from forging connections between the approximately 21 million Muslims in China.

The Times of India in its 11 August 2018 edition reported of a massive protest by Hui Muslims in Weizhou town to demolish the Grand Mosque of Ningxia in Weizhou town. Thousands of ethnic Hui Muslims gathered to thwart the demolition of the mosque in what is said to be one of the largest protests outside Xinjiang. The Chinese government called off demolition until the submission of a new reconstruction plan.

Chinese media had defended the demolition plan saying 'No religion is bigger than law.' Chinese officials also wanted the mosque, which looked like an 'Arab style' mosque with domes from West Asia, should be replaced with Chinese pagodas. The local Muslims had rejected this offer. Clearly, the hard policies in Xinjiang had failed to deter other Muslims in China from protesting. The Chinese government has been relatively soft on Hui Muslims so far. The state's responses to repeated expressions of ethnic minority unrest have oscillated between soft and hard policies. The soft policy approach is exemplified by funding the building and upkeep of mosques.

However, what would be the consequences of this protest remains to be seen in the future, for any similar protest in Xinjiang by Uighur ethnic minorities would have been ruthlessly suppressed by the Chinese government? A United Nations human rights expert panel, as reported in Times of India edition 12 August 2018, has alleged that China was holding two million Uighurs and Muslims in secret camps as 'enemies of the state' based on their religion. The total population of Xinjiang is eleven million. The report said that hundreds of Uighur students who returned from abroad have 'disappeared'.

In his opening address to a UN session in Geneva, Chinese Ambassador to the UN, Yu Jianhua praised China's policies towards minorities, saying they were aimed at promoting unity and harmony. He further said that economic progress in the region had lifted 20 million people out of poverty in the past five years. Tightened security and curbs on religious practices of Uighurs are aimed at preventing violent anti-state activities. This is the standard line of the Communist Party of China on ethnic issues.

Chinese soft power: In a sweeping ironical contrast, thousands of miles away from Beijing, the Chinese Consul General in Kolkata, MA Zhanwu, called a press conference on 17 August 2018 at the iconic The Oberoi Grand Hotel. The stated purpose of the press meet was to project Chinese soft power by announcing the Consulate's association with a local Durga Puja Committee in Salt Lake City to deck up the *puja pandal* with Chinese theme from Yunan province.

A Communist Party of China government official associating with one of India's biggest religious festivals set many people wondering. The Chinese Consul General went to the extent to explain that it was a move to develop 'trust between the two nations.' He further said, 'Goddess Durga is known to many Chinese citizens as "Nan Jin Mu" or the formidable Goddess who can defeat enemies. Images of the Goddess can be seen in several temples in China.' A very different friendly face of the same Chinese government that runs the administrative affairs in XUAR.

Uighur militancy: The Chinese actions in Xinjiang is highlighted in the Western media big time. There is, however, another side of the Xinjiang story. The Uighurs have since the early 1960s, supported by the Soviet Union, come to form its militant wing to take on the Chinese state. The Turkistan Islamic Party is one such group that has openly advocated armed action against China. It is quite similar to the various militant outfits engaging the Indian armed forces in Kashmir in a bloody insurgency.

The Chinese government is well aware of the fact that Uighur militant outfits, based in camps and safe havens in other countries have established an elaborate network with global Islamic terror groups such as Lashkar-e-Taiba, Tehreek-e-Taliban, Islamic State of Iraq, Hizbul

Figure 4.6: MA Zhanwu performing Tai Chi at the Mandap at Salt Lake Puja, Salt Lake BJ Block (Source: India Blooms News Service)

Figure 4.7: MA Zhanwu with the Governor of Bengal at Salt Lake Puja, Salt Lake BJ Block (Source: India Blooms News Service)

Mujahideen, and countless other outfits that pose a global threat to many nations.

Uighur militants have been caught engaging in subversive activities in countries such as Thailand, Indonesia, and Vietnam. The Chinese response to any perceived threat to the state has been firm and fast. China has been vocal in the international fora against global terrorism.

DAY 5

(26 May 2017)

Our fifth-day itinerary in China can be summed as a 'panorama of the past and present.' Our hosts planned a visit to the Great Wild Goose Pagoda and the Xi'an Hi-tech Industries Development Zone. It was like leaping few centuries in a day.

I had informed the organizers in advance about my impending trip to London and they had taken this into account. The delegation was scheduled to stay on for two more days to visit Shanghai and the ancient Chinese town of Zhu Jia Jiao. I excused myself from visiting the Great Wild Goose Pagoda and Xi'an Hi-Tech Industries Development Zone. Instead, I hired a car and headed on my own to visit the pagodas, the Redfort Indian restaurant, and from there to the airport for my return flight to Kolkata via Hong Kong.

One thing that strikes you about Xi'an is its old-world charm. Being a 3,000-year-old city, the contrast with other Chinese cities such as Beijing and Shanghai is obvious. The traffic is less, street vendors, auto-rickshaws and traditional bazaars add to its charm.

The Great Wild Goose Pagoda

This pagoda is an iconic structure of Xi'an, a masterpiece of Buddhist architecture, which stands in the Da Ci'en Temple complex. The Pagoda is rated as a National Key Cultural Relic Preserve and was added to the World UN Heritage list in June 2014 along with the ancient silk road.

A pagoda is found in cultural traditions of Asia. Namely, India, China, Nepal, Vietnam, Sri Lanka as well as far eastern countries like Japan and Korea. The structure is unique with storeys and multiple eaves on the edges.

The Great Wild Goose Pagoda (also called Big Wild Goose Pagoda), a part of the Da Ci'en Temple complex was built in 648 AD to commemorate a dead virtuous queen. The complex covers an area of 5.5 lakh square feet, one-seventh of its original size. It still, however, retains its grandeur and has historically been the seat of Yogacharya school of Buddhist philosophy associated with the Mahayana sect.

A statue of the monk Xuanzang (famous as Hiuen Tsang in India) stands before the temple with guarding lions on both sides of the gate. There are two famous buildings—Bell Tower in the east and Drum Tower in the west—as one enters the temple complex. Along the central axis are the Hall of Mahavira, Sermon Hall, Wild Goose Pagoda, and the Hall of Xuanzang Sanzang.

Also famous as The Giant Wild Goose Pagoda, it is a Buddhist pagoda in the southern part of Xi'an built in 652 AD during the Tang dynasty (618–907 AD). The original structure, built by Emperor Gaozong of Tang (649–83) aka Li Zhi had five storeys. Five more storeys were added in 704 during the reign of Empress Wu Zeitan. The pagoda's exterior brick facade was renovated during the Ming dynasty.

The pagoda was renovated many times during the Ming dynasty. A major earthquake in 1556 heavily damaged the pagoda and reduced it by three storeys to seven storeys. The last major renovation took place in 1964. This 200 feet tall structure of the Pagoda stands there today.

The Great Wild Goose Pagoda offers a panoramic view of the city. Statues of Buddha by famed Tang dynasty artist Yan Liben adorn the walls. Calligraphy further adds to the ambience.

Inside the Great Wild Goose Pagoda, the visitors climb stairs that twists its way up, providing a panorama of the city from the arch-shaped doors on four sides of each storey. On the walls are engraved fine statues of Buddha by the renowned artist Yan Liben of the Tang Dynasty. Steles by noted calligraphers also grace the pagoda.

Speaking of Great Wild Goose Pagoda, one cannot avoid talking about Empress Wu who was one of the most ruthless and efficient ladies to leave her footprints in the Chinese history dominated by men.

Empress Wu Zeitan: Empress Wu was the concubine of Emperor Taizong and married his ninth son Emperor Gaozong. After the sudden death of Gaozong she went on to rule as Empress regnant. Empress Wu had an affair with a Buddhist monk Huaiyi in 685 and he was bestowed with great honours and favours but later they fell out and Huaiyi was killed.

In 690 AD, Wu took the final step to become the empress regnant of the newly proclaimed Zhou dynasty and took the title of *Huangdi*. Shortly after Wu took the throne, she elevated the status of Buddhism above that of Taoism, officially sanctioning Buddhism by building Dayun temples and appointing nine senior monks as dukes.

Empress Wu welcomed Chinese traveller Yijhing (known as I-Tsing in India) in 695 AD after he returned from Srivijaya (Sumatra) and India after a 25-year sojourn. He brought back some 400 Buddhist translated texts. Yijhing was a great admirer of earlier Buddhist monks and travellers, Fa-Hien and Xuanzang.

The Great Wild Goose Temple became one of the three largest text-translating centres of ancient China.

Xuanzang (Hiuen Tsang): Xuanzang was born in 602 AD and became a Buddhist monk at the age of 20. Of the pagoda's many functions was to hold *sutra*s and figurines of the Buddha.

Xuanzang brought these to China from India after an arduous 19 year journey during which he kept a journal of his unique experiences and observations which later came to be known as Hsi-yu Chi. He is described as Hiuen Tsang, the 'Prince of Pilgrims,' in history books. He, along with his predecessor Buddhist monk Fa-Hien, are the two most famous Chinese travellers in the history of Indo-China relations. However, the historical contribution of Xuanzang, with regard to India and China, is far more than his predecessor.

Xuanzang had a burning desire to know more about Buddhism. He knew his spiritual quest could be fulfilled only by undertaking a trip to India. It was against the laws in those days to travel abroad, so he secretly left China when he was about 30 for an adventurous journey towards India.

Xuanzang started off from Chang'an (ancient Xi'an), along the Silk Road, and reached India—the cradle of Buddhism—after passing through the central Asiatic regions of Turfa, Karshahr, Tashkent, Samarkand, and Bactria, surviving the rigours of forbidding deserts and rugged mountains. He narrowly escaped death many times. He finally entered India in 631 AD by crossing the Hindu Kush into Kapisa after visiting 34 kingdoms along the way.

Xuanzang traveled extensively across hundreds of provinces and regions for 17 years. He stayed in India for 14 years covering northern and southern India. He wanted to visit all the sacred places connected with the life of Buddha. He visited Kapilavastu, Bodh-Gaya, Sarnath, and Kusinagara. He also traveled through the Deccan, Orissa, and Bengal. He went almost to every part of India including Kashmir and Punjab.

He spent around five years in the University of Nalanda and studied there. He was impressed by the passion of the Indian people towards learning. He was a keen observer and compiler of facts. He keenly observed the social, religious, political, cultural, and economic conditions of India.

At that time, Pataliputra had lost its former glory and Kanauj and Prayag had become important cities of learning. King Harsha admired Xuanzang's deep devotion to Buddha and his profound knowledge of Buddhism. He honored him in his Kanauj religious Assembly and also invited him to attend the Prayaga Assembly. After attending those two magnificent functions, he left for China.

King Harshavardhana was sorry having to part with the pilgrim and made elaborate arrangements for his safe return under a strong military escort to the frontiers of India. Beyond the frontiers, the pilgrim was accompanied by Harsha's official guides who carried the letters of authority from the emperor to produce them in other countries. Xuanzang returned to China safely.

Xuanzang brought with him from India 150 pieces of the bodily relics of Buddha, a large number of Buddha images in gold, silver and sandalwood and above all, 657 volumes of *sutras* and valuable manuscripts that were carried by 20 horses of his escort party.

Back in China, he set himself to translate some of those manuscripts into the Chinese language, assisted by several scholars. About 74 Buddhist works were translated during his lifetime which proved of immense value to the people of China.

As the first abbot of Da Ci'en Temple, Xuanzang got the permission of Emperor Gaozong and supervised the building of the pagoda inside it. He got the Sanskrit *sutras* translated into Chinese totaling 1,330 volumes, which heralded a new era in the history of translation. He also wrote a book on his journey to India titled Pilgrimage to the West. Scholars have attached great importance to his work. Xuanzang died in 664 AD.

His visit to India was an important event of the reign of King Harshavardhana. India is much indebted to this Chinese traveller for the valuable accounts he left behind sharing political, religious, economic, social conditions of those days. He also wrote the details of India in China and was under no compulsion to flatter anyone, that is why his works are considered an authentic account of his travels.

Many of the treasures that made the Great Wild Goose Pagoda famous were lost during the Cultural Revolution in China. Others are kept away from public view. There are many featured squares and gardens around the Great Wild Goose Pagoda and Da Ci'en temple, which provides the locals and tourists with wonderful resorts for free. The most remarkable one should be the North Square boasting the largest musical fountain in Asia.

Besides, the Tang Ci'en Temple Site Park and the Shaanxi Opera Garden to the east, the Shaanxi Folk Customs Garden to the west, as well as the South Square with the statue of Xuanzang and the Great Tang All Day Mall to the south are also worth visiting.

On 14 May 2015, Indian Prime Minister Narendra Modi visited China but his itinerary was somewhat unusual. The first stop or arrival was Xi'an and not Beijing. This had surprised many. Even more surprising was the fact that Chinese President Xi Jinping travelled to Xi'an to welcome Modi. The first such gesture for any foreign leader. The Chinese news agency Xinhua said, 'Xi'an was a carefully orchestrated choice.'

Xi'an is also President Xi Jinping's hometown and when Xi visited India in September 2014, he had first gone to Gujarat, Modi's home turf, before going to New Delhi. It was obvious Xi paid back the courtesy by visiting Xi'an for Modi.

Modi and Xi had also visited the Great Wild Goose Pagoda together. Referring to a gift received at the pagoda of a figurine of Xuanzang and a framed Buddha with the message: 'Water The Friendship Between India and China With Oriental Wisdom,' Prime Minister Modi had tweeted 'Always appreciate this token of appreciation.'

Redfort Indian restaurant

I came to know about Redfort Restaurant and Club, an Indian restaurant located on Silk Road Street in Xi'an and decided to pay a visit. It is a chain of Indian restaurant which popularizes the concept or theme of being a 'cultural restaurant.'

The Redfort Restaurant and Club offers a wide range of vegetarian and non-vegetarian delicious Indian cuisine. The ambience is inspired by the Red Fort in Delhi and there is an outdoor sitting facility with free WiFi services. The restaurants double up as a centre for a yoga studio and Bollywood dance centre which celebrates Holi, Yoga Day, Chinese New Year, and other festivals that are cultural hallmarks of the two countries. It also conducts 'yogashala' workshops and Bollywood dance sessions.

Figure 5.1: Author at the Indian Pavilion

As I approached the Redfort Indian restaurant, I saw a huge idol of Lord Ganesha. I came to know that the local government has made pavilions of various countries such as India, Korea, Japan, Russia, and so on. Each pavilion presented the local handicraft, shops, eateries, and so on.

The India pavilion had an Indian handicraft and goods shop called Amber, a dried-fruit shop and a yoga studio as well. Interestingly, all owned by the Chinese. Inside the Indian pavilion, they have also created few structures depicting scenes of Ramayana and Mahabharat.

From the first bite, I knew the quality of the food at the Redfort Restaurant and Club was very good. And it

Figure 5.2: Indian Pavilion

Figure 5.3: Indian food at Redfort

only got better. In a recent interview on ten best overseas restaurants serving authentic Indian food, I recommended Redfort Restaurant and Club.

I found it a little difficult to reach this restaurant because the complex it is housed in has quite a few entrances. Thanks to Kartak Singh Rana, my knight in shining armour, who came to the main road to pick me up.

I agree with the saying 'fewer the Indians, stronger the bonding.' Kartak Singh Rana told me that this Redfort Restaurant has been on since 2012. Among many things, Kartak mentioned the high-level security check they all had to go through during Prime Minister Modi's visit.

The restaurant is owned by Dev Raturi who is popular by his Chinese name De Fu. He is the co-founder and Chief Executive Officer (CEO) of Redfort Group China. He came to China in 2005 when he was 29 to learn *kung fu* and martial art. He started as a waiter in an Indian restaurant to make a living. Now he runs four Indian restaurants, two

Chinese restaurants and one French restaurant in cities such as Xi'an, Hangzhou, Chengdu, and Beijing. He is also planning to start 'Chen Cheng' (Great Wall of China) chain of Chinese restaurants in India. He lives in Xi'an with his wife Anjali and two children.

Dev or De Fu promotes Indian culture through yoga workshops and Bollywood dancing in Xi'an. He also holds Holi and Chinese New Year celebrations where Indians and Chinese intermingle. He has started India International Yoga Studio in China. He has acted in movies and got a fair share of publicity in Chinese media.

Rana's journey to China has been a little different. In 2000, he worked in Punjabi By Nature Restaurant in Delhi. He came to Shanghai in 2005. He came to Xi'an in 2013. Rana reminds me of managers and restaurateurs I have met at the Indian restaurants in offbeat locations. Indians have proved their mettle outside India through hard work and entrepreneurial zeal. Time and again Indians have proved their ability to adjust to the difficult situations on foreign soil.

I have witnessed Indian cooks from Himachal Pradesh to South India in Malaysia; plumbers and carpenters from Rajasthan working in the Gulf; thriving Sindhi communities in Latin American countries. After a good meal at the Hava Mahal where you can get *samosas* and *pyaz pakora* (onion fries) packed, I left for the airport. I thanked Kartak Rana Singh for his affection and being a friend-in-need.

I learned quite a lot from my five-day visit to China, but I was moved by the kind souls such as Bharat and Gita. Next on our delegation agenda was an official visit to the XHTZ—Xi'an's 'Silicon Valley' or 'China's Bangalore.'

Xi'an Hi-Tech Industries and Development Zone (XHTZ)

Xi'an Hi-tech Industries Development Zone (XHTZ) is located on the southern outskirts of Xi'an, 7 kilometres to the city downtown area and 7 kilometres from the urban centre. The Hi-tech Zone was established in 1991.

There are 114 such hi-tech zones across China. These are also known as the Chinese science parks and XHTZ is regarded as one of the most successful hi-tech zones and is one of the five national model science parks and the first one to join the network of sci-tech industrial parks of APEC member countries.

In 2002, the United Nations Industrial Development Organization (UNIDO) recognized it as one of the six most vigorous urban zones in China.

In 2014, the State Intellectual Property Office evaluated and selected the Xi'an Hi-tech Industries Development Zone as a national intellectual property demonstration zone. It is a governmental recognition for its efforts to promote the development of high-tech industries with proprietary intellectual property rights. China aims to turn XHTZ into an innovation hub for science and a research and development base for new age scientific enterprises and emerging high technology industries.

China's Bangalore: One of the key projects of XHTZ is the New Software Park or China's Bangalore. The focus would be on information technology and high-tech services, mobile Internet, cloud computing, e-commerce, Internet of Things, software R&D, integrated applications, navigation applications, service outsourcing, data centre, R&D and design, creative industries and headquarters economy, and so on.

Over a thousand capital enterprises, including many Global 500 companies from the US, UK, Germany, Japan, South Korea, Singapore, Taiwan, and Hong Kong, have settled in the zone. It has received over 20 visiting heads of states and dignitaries. It is one of those success stories on a gargantuan scale.

Tourism in China—Red Guards to Red Tourism

One thing that struck me during my brief visit to China was the Chinese officials and their meticulous planning. The manner they extended their hospitality to foreign dignitaries called for a great degree of preparation and expertise. A fusion of homework and government strategy.

There was no tourism during the Mao Zedong era in China. Today, tourism is very profitable and booming.

Nearly 100 million Chinese travel abroad each year. A lot more travel within China.

Though late, China has realized that its reservoir of ancient legacy, or what remains of it, is nothing less than a jackpot. It can attract global tourists and revenues in a big way. Ironically, much of that legacy was ruined during Mao Zedong's Cultural Revolution (1966–76) when 13 million Mao-inspired students, even school children—the Red Guards—destroyed innumerable ancient temples, ancient structures, shrines, books, paintings, drawings, relics, artifacts, and anything 'old' they could lay their hands on.

Old cultures, including religious customs of minorities in Tibet and Xingjiang, were destroyed in right earnest. Six thousand monasteries were destroyed in Tibet alone. Red Guards burned sacred writings from the Quran and shut down Islamic sites in Xingjiang. The damage was colossal, the loss incalculable.

In a strange twist of fate, Chiang Kai-shek's retreating army stole over 6 lakhs work of art from the Imperial Palace and brought it to Taiwan. Today, many of those treasured artifacts are exhibited in Taiwan's National Palace Museum and can be visited by tourists from mainland China.

China's Communist Leader, Mao Zedong launched the Great Proletarian Cultural Revolution on August 6, 1966, to assert his authority over the government after his position weakened in the Communist Party due to the failure of his Great Leap Forward (1958–60) and the ensuing economic crisis. The Cultural Revolution, as it is widely known, had many phases and lasted for 10 years.

Mao came to believe that leaders of the Communist Party of China were moving the nation in a wrong direction. Mao called upon the youth to purge the 'impure elements' of Chinese society and revive the revolutionary spirit that had led to the victory in War. The violent legacy unleashed tormented China for decades.

Mao's call for youth mobilization gave birth to the formation of Red Guards, a paramilitary group comprising young students who turned against the 'intellectual' elderly members of the Party. Mao unleashed the young groups on the senior members of the Party who often criticized his views. Mao instructed the Red Guards to do away with old ideas, old customs, old culture and old habits.

The Red Guards unleashed a brutal attack on teachers, officials, cadres or anyone who was perceived to be an intellectual clinging to the traditional values. Thousands were killed, maimed, tortured, and humiliated while educational institutions closed down and theatres and films were banned. Soon different factions within the Red Guards emerged, vying for dominance and control, bringing China to the brink of civil war and anarchy. When the situation spiralled out of control, Mao had to summon the People's Liberation Army to combat the Red Guards.

The Cultural Revolution lasted a decade till 1976, causing untold sufferings and miseries to millions of Chinese.

The death toll was estimated closed to two million and incalculable loss of cultural heritage.

From 1980 onward, the Chinese government under Deng Xiaoping, who was himself purged twice during the Cultural Revolution, gradually began to restore the monuments and revive cultural sites. In 1985, China signed the UN Convention on World Heritage and three years later established the State Bureau to preserve Chinese culture and heritage.

Today, China has come a long way since the days of the Red Guards. What can best be described as the law of unintended consequences, every year, millions of Chinese visit the mausoleum of Mao Zedong—one of the greatest iconoclast of Chinese culture—at the Tiananmen Square.

The Chinese government allows religious beliefs, traditions and customs as long as they do not conflict with the principles of the Communist Party. Which parts of old Chinese culture are worth reviving is an ongoing ideological debate within China.

The damage done during the Cultural Revolution cannot be undone. Today's Chinese government is trying to retrieve, revive or preserve whatever is possible. This is driven by the twin objectives. First, to monetize the national assets through tourism. Second, to use tourism as a political tool to reconcile two conflicting ideas rooted in the revolutionary past and the evolutionary present.

The conflict is: How to maintain the relevance of the revolutionary history of the Communist Party to a new generation of Chinese raised on commercial pop culture, consumerism and digital social media? The answer is Red Tourism.

Red Tourism: It is a state-sponsored program to encourage travel to historical sites in China related to the Chinese Communist Revolution. The Chinese government has set up Red Tourism (RT) sites across China. These sites are places associated with the key and decisive happenings of the Communist movement in China. Like the founding of the Chinese Communist Party, the formation of Red Army, Long March, War of Resistance against Japan, Mao's personal life experiences and so on.

RT sites are linked to tourist circuits and try to foist the revolutionary memory or spirit of the state on the people. Red Tourism is an ideological tool that involves singing, dancing, reciting Communist pledges, dressing in Red Army uniforms, eating 'revolutionary food' and selfies.

One such RT site is Liangjiahe where President Xi Jinping spent several years in his youth during the Cultural Revolution. Another more famous RT site is Jinggangshan where Mao and Zhu De are said to have selflessly carried grains for their soldiers. Many tours to these sites are organized by schools and private organizations.

Some of the management institutes such as Beijing Huashang Institute of Management (BHIM), Peking University and Jucheng China, offer Maoism Management Classes. BHIM conducts trips to Jianggangshan for an educational experience for its students—the future businessmen and entrepreneurs of

China. Many people in China believe that visits to RT sites can bring all kinds of benefits, from perks to promotions to unseen privileges.

China and India

China and India have a long way to go. The world's two most populated countries have their advantages and weaknesses. I don't know if the two can work for a common goal, but if both the countries can come together, it will perhaps be the world's most powerful alliance.

It had been a long day and I soon dozed off once I perched myself comfortably in the Dragon Airways seat. When I woke up, I saw an airhostess smiling with a hot towel. She said we were about to land soon. I peered out the window, Kolkata was racing up to welcome me.

EPILOGUE

A five-day trip to any country can be an eye-opener. And when it is China there is always a lot more than what meets the eye.

Many commentators in Delhi felt that India would be isolated and lose out by turning its back on the BRI. However, India's stand to oppose BRI seems to be vindicated by the turn of global events. The European Union has echoed India's concern that BRI lacks transparency and refused to back Xi Jinping's BRI-related trade statement.

The BRI project to connect Asia, Europe and Africa, projected at USD 8 trillion, has started to hit roadblocks. There is a growing realization among the poor countries that Chinese proposal to build massive infrastructure projects come at an extremely high price. Many partner states are re-negotiating deals and in many cases, entire projects have been called off. Even Pakistan, China's all-weather-friend, has downgraded some projects.

The reason? China's debt trap diplomacy!

The plight of countries in a debt trap is like that of a poor farmer giving away his daughter to the cruel moneylender.

According to a study by the Centre for Global Development, of the possible 68 BRI partner countries, 23 have the risk of debt distress. BRI projects have left a mountain of debts that countries are unable to service. News of more countries trapped in the dragon's deadly debt embrace keeps coming in.

The spectacular growth story of China has now begun to lose its shine with the slowing of the economy, rising labor costs, ageing labor force and an impending trade war with the United States at its doorstep. Add to this the ominous signs of making of an all-powerful personality cult around president Xi, reminiscent of the Gang of Four. Chinese debt trap ticks off when dream projects turn out to be white elephants.

By drawing a rosy picture of growth and profitability, China offers high-interest loans to countries for infrastructure projects. The Chinese government insists on government-to-government deals. The terms and conditions of these 'dream projects' are never made public and international competition for the project is eliminated. High-interest loans are passed off as investments and only Chinese companies get the contracts for executing the projects. While the Chinese get paid for their loans through contracts, the countries are saddled with debts to repay. Though the local unemployment may be very high, only Chinese labour is used in the projects.

When the projects fail to generate the perceived revenues, the country slowly slides into a debt trap. Unable to repay the debts, the countries have no choice but to pledge and fritter away their national assets to the Chinese, often in the form of a 99-year lease of land. Sri Lanka's Hambantota port is one such classic example. Another Chinese project in Sri Lanka is dubbed as the 'world's emptiest international airport.'

Sri Lanka owes USD 8 billion to the state-controlled Chinese firms. Nearly 95 per cent of all government revenues are for debt servicing. China has acquired a geo-strategic naval outpost in the Indian Ocean and alarmed India, Japan, and Australia. Using similar tactics, China has acquired a naval outpost in Djibouti, which is also the base of US military operations in Africa.

This modus operandi to expand the Chinese zone of influence internationally has military implications with potential flashpoints. The perception that China is using investments and loans to snatch up ports and other assets of a country is damaging its earlier carefully cultivated soft power image.

Malaysian Prime Minister Mahathir Mohammad during his visit to Beijing in August 2018 minced no words standing at the Great Hall of the People to highlight international concerns of Chinese using geo-economic tools to achieve geopolitical ends.

Mahathir announced cancellation of USD 23 billion worth of Chinese projects in Malaysia. Sierra Leone has scrapped a USD 318 million airport deal. Pakistan, Nepal and Myanmar have scrapped or sidelined three major hydroelectric projects worth USD 20 billion planned by Chinese companies. Pakistan cited tough financing terms imposed by China for cancelling USD 14 billion Diamer-Bhasha hydroelectric dam project. Nepal has called off USD 2.5 billion dam project due to financial irregularities on the part of Chinese companies. Myanmar cancelled a USD 3.6 billion dam project three years ago and has said it is no longer interested in big hydro-electric projects.

Countries such as Mongolia, Venezuela, Djibouti, Montenegro, Cameroon, Laos, Cambodia, Tajikistan, Krygystan, Maldives, Pacific island states of Nauru, Vanuatu, and others have a huge debt to repay after implementing Chinese projects. Because of the various infrastructure projects, Laos and Cambodia now owe huge debts due to China and their status dubbed as wholly owned subsidiaries of China. International Monetary Fund has warned that Chinese loans are promoting unsustainable debt burdens.

'Vulnerable countries are awakening to the risks of accepting loans that are too good to be true and then slipping into debt entrapment. China is even replicating some of the practices that were used against it during European colonial period, such as the concept of a 99-year lease,' wrote Brahma Chellany in The Times of India's 29 October 2018 edition.

The Sino-US trade war amid a slowing economy is a matter of deep concern for China. The trade war moved a notch up with the US targeting Chinese state-owned company by restricting American companies from selling crucial software and technology. The ban could bring the company to its knees. A similar US move against Chinese telecommunications equipment maker in April 2018 brought its factories to a standstill for months.

The Trump administration has said China's effort to get hold of American technology is an 'existential threat' to the future of the US economy. It has made the issue a central part of its trade fight with Beijing, imposing tariffs on USD 250 billion of Chinese goods and threatening more unless Beijing changes its industrial policies. This could be a big setback for Beijing's 'Made in China—2025' plan to attain self-sufficiency in hi-tech industries by 2025.

The internal development in China is a matter of concern for China itself. In January 2018, senior Chinese Communist Party officials gathered for a two-day session behind closed doors to take a decision—abolish presidential term limits to allow Xi Jinping to hold power indefinitely. A 35-year-old provision of China's constitution that allowed two terms of five years each to the President and Vice President was swiftly amended with no discussions or deliberations. A political convention that had for decades helped shield China from succession struggles was demolished.

This move by Xi Jinping was nothing less than a constitutional coup and perhaps marked the advent of a new personality cult in China. Xi had used the anti-corruption investigation tool to silence his rivals and any potential opposition.

Xi, who came to power in 2013, has concentrated more power than any other Chinese leader since Mao Zedong. A strong Xi could mean a weaker Chinese Communist Party. Censoring news in mainstream and social media, ideological purification of academia and surveillance of general masses raises the bogey of Big Brother sitting atop the Great Chinese Digital Wall watching and purging every move of citizens that is considered to be against the state. This would justify the fact that the Chinese state budget devotes more resources to internal security than national defense.

How does all this affect India remains to be seen. With Mr Narendra Modi back in power, India's successful policy of presenting itself as a counter-weight to China in the region should get a boost.